SURVIVIN'
IT'S JUST WHAT WE DO!
Leslie D. Walker

Print ISBN: 978-1-09835-342-1
eBook ISBN: 978-1-09835-343-8

Some simple notes on how to #SURVIVE your kids, their school and life along with all the other people, places and things that may seem to get in your way as you are trying to do it all and keep it together. Raising kids in Miami, Florida is quite the experience for us all and will have you questioning your every move because image is everything regardless of where you are, home, school, work or even the grocery store!

This book is dedicated to my four beautiful children! Thank you to my amazing friends who inspired me to write this comedic memoir based on my own crazy experiences combined with their hilarious experiences. Without you ladies swapping stories with me via endless phone calls and texts about our kids, our crazy days at work and home, along with the power of social media to connect us all, this would not be happening. Thank you all for allowing me to be the MOM I know how to be and supporting me in who I am as I support you all in who you are, Bad Ass Moms just #SURVIVIN'!

CONTENTS

THRIVIN' AND SURVIVIN'

CONGRATULATIONS! WELCOME TO PARENTHOOD! WHAT a beautiful time in our lives! That moment that we became not only a parent but a MOMMY! It is so surreal and so amazing to experience! The wonderful memories we all share as parents about the day we became responsible for someone other than ourselves! It was such a great and special day for me becoming a mommy, and I am sure you all felt the same way when you had your first baby. The feeling doesn't really leave when babies two, three, four, and so on, are delivered via stork, but that first-time feeling is so special, that nothing can really replace the day you became a parent. Regardless of it was your first time or fifth time, it was the best feeling ever to know that we have someone who will love us unconditionally and will never fault us when we are having a bad day!

How it felt to hold my little baby for the first time was so incredible! It felt like a million clouds had swept me away to an alternate universe that only me and my little bundle would enjoy together. No one could bring me down to earth because I was in heaven just watching her sleep, eat, poop, cry, smile, move, or just simply breathe. The hundreds of candid shots taken on day one are some of the best memories that you will have to reflect on this joyous time in your life. The endless visits to the hospital and/or to your home by family and friends, make you feel so loved and cared for by those who know you best—is such a great feeling to have.

Living in Miami, Florida, appearance can weigh on you and cause unwarranted stress. I didn't care about having bad hair days, or days with no make-up. I was more concerned about picking out the cutest onesie and matching socks and hat so that I could start playing dress-up with the baby.

It reminded me of playing with my very own baby dolls back in the day. Those ten little toes and ten little fingers, the deep dimples, the rosy cheeks and beautiful light brown or green eyes below that luscious curly head of hair, are some of our many reasons for endless kisses, stares and snuggles. The smells of "new baby" are everywhere! We are in baby heaven and mommy bliss! Nothing can take us off this cloud, and we were not even worried about coming down. Just being with our baby is all we need at that moment! Heaven on earth is the best description.

The sleepless nights and long days are beautiful! The countless laundry baskets and diaper pails are unforgettable! Let's not forget the projectile vomit and diarrhea keeps us in awe of why we love being a parent! Yeah, those first twelve months are a breeze! Nobody talks back to you and nobody understands how to roll their eyes yet! It's a beautiful beginning. To top off such an incredible year of parenthood and baby love, we celebrate with a grand, over the top, First Birthday Party. Everyone is invited to the big soiree, which includes the entire neighborhood, every mommy and daddy at the mommy-n-me or daddy-n-me play groups, every family member who can make it along with your friends and co-workers. They are all there with you to celebrate this special moment. The first birthday is always so much fun for everyone, except the baby. They don't care about the balloons, bouncy house, food, games or the people invited. They are there for food, sleep and deposits. They are usually tired and cranky at least two hours in. They are crying because they are being continuously passed around to everyone who is not mommy, daddy, nana or gramps, or being picked up, which is really interrupting either a well-needed nap or some serious cake eating.

When all of the partying is over and the troops have all retreated to their respective homes, you take that time to reflect on Year one, all while putting that precious baby to bed for the night. Tomorrow is the start of year two, and you just know that it will be as great as year one has been, smooth sailing on all fronts (disclaimer: if this is your first baby, that is what you think; if this is not the first baby, you are not easily fooled). Your baby will just continue to follow directions, they will continue to take naps anytime you put them down for one, they will be everything that you have dreamed about or read about in one of those "new moms" self-help books. Day 365 is over and Day one of Round two is upon us.

Year two starts off just as year one ended, smoothly, and all is well in your world. No major changes have been noticed, no shake-ups in moods or movements. Nothing seems to be different quite yet. If we fast forward into Year two about three to six months, things start to get a little different. You seem to have a shorter patience than normal, nothing to ring the alarm about, but something to keep an eye on. You notice that you have started exhibiting behaviors that do not reflect any behaviors from Year one. For example, you start cursing under your breath when someone calls your phone during nap time or comes over unannounced and rings that damn doorbell. You seem to keep more dishes in the sink than usual, and the diaper genie is really more annoying than you thought, and you can't understand why you asked for it on the registry. You seem to keep your hair up more and your shoes may go from four-inch stilettos to running shoes while at home or anywhere other than your office or workplace. Your purse is starting to look more like a diaper bag filled with cups, binkies, wipes and toys, than it is filled with your favorite lipstick, powder and even your wallet. You only carry your license and credit card with you when you head out, and your Starbucks app has a major decrease in points earned.

Some of us went back to work after six weeks, some of us went back at six months and some of us had the luxury of going back after a year. No matter when we go back to work, we have a plan that consists of kicking ass and taking names later, unless it involves our baby. Working and Momin' isn't easy, but we don't stress because we know "It's handled!" Around the fifteen to eighteen-month mark, you are still trying to be that put-together working mom who can do it all. You have scheduled playdates (for an eighteen-month-old). You have told yourself a million times over, you can do this, and everything is fine. If you are still on baby one, you are a force to be reckoned with.

If this is baby two or more, you are on a totally different route. You notice that the twenty-four hours that are allotted in a day don't seem to be working out for you every day; but some days, maybe most days, you are killing it. You are SURVIVIN', and everyone who is everyone notices.

After a few discussions with other mommies at the park or other mommies at work, you find yourself looking into half-day—or shall I be real and say 2½ hour—preschools. You have been brainwashed to think and believe that putting your precious baby into "preschool" will not only give your baby a head start in the education department, but it is so good for their social and emotional development. Insert disclaimer: If this is baby one, we understand how you were pulled in; but if this is baby two or more, YOU KNOW BETTER!

Let's take a quick moment and talk about this "preschool." We all know we didn't sign our kids up just to enhance their social skills, we signed their asses up because either everyone else was doing it and we didn't want to be left out, or we found out that for those 2½ hours we can have a small amount of peace and quiet. Well that only applies if you have one kid, but if you have multiple kids, whoever can go is going, and it at least makes those 2½ hours a lot calmer. Yes, it's only 2 ½ hours, which to any parent who needs a break seems like forever, but in reality, we sometimes only need a few moments to breathe and think again. This very expensive-ass playdate, which is what I have chosen to call it after I have been bamboozled three kids later, is a small piece of sanity that I will not ever knock any parent from experiencing if it can be afforded. I encourage it. It kept me sane. It kept me from being on the five o'clock news. It kept me alive! If for those three reasons alone doesn't encourage any mommy to look into this scam, then I don't know if I can help you any longer.

Year two is winding down and things are even more different than expected. Your kid starts to tell you "NO!" It's cute at first, until you start to see your in-laws laugh when they say it, so the bouncy toddler says it again! That stage when your beautiful baby boy gets into the flour and throws it all over your kitchen. When your darling baby girl gets into your make-up and decides to "color mama" on your white walls with mascara! When your set of multiples think it's soooo fun to take off their diapers and run through the house naked and unafraid of the dark brown S%!T staining your white carpet! Those are the moments that we say are priceless and unforgettable, but at the same time we believe the devil is trying to lay his eyes upon our children and prey! We have to keep telling ourselves that these children are our little angels sent from Heaven to guide us and provide us with everlasting love and affection. In reality. we realize—or shall I say we start to believe—that these children are out to get us, that they formed a secret society after birth in the nursery. We start to question at this stage, if this is our first child, am I ready for baby number two? Or do I dare say, am I ready for baby number three or four? And if multiples run in your family, like they do in mine, do you even try again with the unknowing fear that the first set of twins could turn into the triplets, or let's face it, any number over zero!? My friends, if you can #SURVIVE year one, you will #SURVIVE THE NEXT eighteen! Trust me. I did so, I know you can too!

SURVIVIN' "PK" VERSUS "AK"

FIRST LET'S TALK PK (PRE-KIDS) WHEN WE ARE ALWAYS put together. This will be brief, as I have very little memory of these amazing times. During the PK time, we know what we want, what we need and when we need it! Our closets are full of fresh-pressed clothing, all in color order or some type of organized fashion. Our shoes are tastefully placed and in a grand order. Some of us even have that Carrie Bradshaw closet and we are so proud of it. The morning routine is just that, a routine. We get up, we may have a favorite song we get up to—you know some Queen Bey, JLo or maybe even Cardi B. We get up, we dance, we are feeling ourselves and loving every single inch of our bodies and we don't care who is watching. We get dressed, get our hair and face all the way together. You know, get them eyebrows all the way arched, mascara is on point and our powder game is one for the God's people. I'm talking, we are serving all the milk to bring the boys to the yard. If you are married, you are just making sure your boy is always in your yard!

The door opens and we are literally, NYFW strutting out the door on time. Once that car door is open, we get in, we pull down that visor mirror and give ourselves a nice smile and say, We Got This! We hit reverse and out the driveway we go. Once we start moving, the music gets down deep in our soul! We are really feeling ourselves at this point. We have our shades on, sunroof is open, air is on, because we refuse to let the humidity ruin this nice hair and make-up. We pull into our favorite drive thru, Starbucks, Dunkin Donuts maybe even McDonald's. Heading to the office we are looking and feeling great. Smiling from ear to ear, not because we love our jobs, but because we feel amazing and ready to tackle the day! We get into work and ·

do our thang. The hours fly by, lunch comes and goes and before you know it, it's time to get off. At this time, we are trying to determine what we are having for dinner. Do I cook? Should we go out to eat? Should it be take-out and we eat at home? The idea that we actually have the time to really think about this subject with such detail doesn't seem like it will ever be foreign to us. We are living in the moment, and it's great!

Once we are home, we eat dinner in peace and quiet. We watch our DVR without interruption. We walk around our home with ease and uninterrupted routines. Bath time consists of candles and wine. We relax in our bathrooms like it is a freaking five-star day spa. The house is clean. The dishes are put away. Tomorrow's outfit is ready and waiting for you to jump into and slay! You head to your room, grab your electronics and relax. Whether that is reading a book on your Kindle, playing Candy Crush on your iPad, scrolling through Facebook and Instagram to stalk your friends and family on your phone or just browse the internet on our laptop. You are lying in your bed, comfortable and with enough space to move about as much and as far as you would like. To top it off, if you are in the "mood," you have hours and hours of uninterrupted, mind-blowing, relations with your significant other! Life as you know it at this point is great and presents no need for concern or panic. You fall asleep and stay asleep for your full eight hours. You get up refreshed and ready to start your day!

Now let's get real and talk about the days AK (After Kids)! This, my friend, is the beginning of the rest of your life—well, at least until they are out of your house and you are no longer responsible for them on a day-to-day basis with feeding, clothing and bathing! After your first baby, you do whatever you can to stay the course. You do your best to get dressed daily, brush your teeth, do your hair and so forth. This may last for a few weeks, maybe even a few months, but if you are anything like me, it lasted only a few weeks. As the kids kept coming, this phase of looking and feeling my best were gone! I tried as a young mom to keep it up all while learning all of this baby stuff. I was exhausted trying to keep up appearances and shit. It was too much for this mama, but some of you may be better than me. To each their own, this is a no-judgement zone! It got to the point where I was answering the door looking like I was cast in American Horror Story. I mean the only thing I know for sure I did daily was brush my teeth. That, my friend, is a must!

The morning comes quickly, AK. It seems like you closed your eyes and five seconds later your baby alive came ALIVE! The calling your name from down the hall, the crying that you hear over the baby monitor or the little pitter-patter of feet walking down the hallway, YOU ARE UP! Sleep is overrated anyway, right? Let's not forget that this wake-up is roughly around five or six a.m. You only closed your eyes literally two hours ago because you were awakened by crying from a little person and no other adult in the house seemed to hear it but you. Strange, right?

Morning routines are really, really different AK compared to PK. The only dancing you may be doing in the morning will be because you don't have all three kids up at once. This is cause for a very silent celebration. You are listening to Queen Bey in your head and making baby moves like Cardi B makes money moves. You are rushing to get outfits out and ready. Some may need ironing; some may need to just be packed in the diaper bag for accident purposes. Some may just be the second outfit of the morning because the first has already been soiled by something. Breakfast is getting burned, bottles are getting made, book bags are being packed, hair is being brushed and lunches are being thrown together.

Remember when I said PK you know what you want, what you need and when you need it? Well AK, you have no idea anymore of what you want, you barely remember what you need, and you have zero fucking time to remember when you needed it by. Let's break a few subjects down to address this non-existent theme of life. We shall start with the dreaded monthly cycle. We know it comes each month. We know how it starts and how it ends symptoms-wise. We know what is working for us flow-wise, and we try very very hard to make sure we have the appropriate supplies.

I have a question for you mamas out there. Have you ever been so frazzled and just done with the day, that when you remember that your monthly is on the way, you rush to the store and grab what you "think" is your regular go-to and when you get home, it turns out that it was not what you thought it was? Well I thought this only happened to me, and then after swapping stories with my friends I learned that I was not alone. I went to Target to grab my usual monthly supply. I rush down the aisle because I know that I only have a limited window of opportunity to get what I need to #SURVIVE because it's nap time or Nana is over for a while. Once I get home, I just throw that shit under my sink and move on with my day. The red sea finally parts and the floodgates open. I reach under my sink and what to my wondering eyes should appear… is not anything I recognize. Why do I have Poise Pads? I do not have a leaky bladder that I am aware of at this point in my life. Please God, don't tell me I grabbed bladder pads instead of period pads! I have no back-ups unless I grab a pull-up diaper at this point. I ain't got time for this shit, so let us Pray and see if these bladder pads can hold a few pints of blood. I refuse to go back to Target at eight p.m., I have shit to do. I will deal with that tomorrow.

Our significant others should have a tight grasp on when it's on the way and what we are craving, what sets us off and what makes us happy during this five to seven-day period. For some strange reason, they get amnesia and start asking us why we are crying all day, why we are eating so much chocolate or drinking sodas and why we have such an attitude about everything.

WTF, first off, my fucking stomach feels like it has been hit by a Mack truck over and over again for hours without pause. Second, my vagina is bleeding constantly, and it seems to get heavier and heavier by the fucking second. Third, I can't seem to go to the bathroom alone to take care of my needs without little people following me asking me, "What's that, mommy?" Lastly, did I feed you three fucking meals today? Have YOUR kids been fed and cleaned? Did you enjoy your Klondike Bar and Blue Moon without

YOUR mini-me asking you for some all while putting their dirty-ass hands on your ice cream bar and being a savage? The answer to all of those questions is YES. Yes, you had three good-ass meals today—all gourmet, may I add. Yes, YOUR kids have been fed and thoroughly bathed. Yes, you enjoyed your snack alone and in peace, so right now, Go find someone else to fuck with at this point. I am not the one right now. Leave me be for five to seven days and all things will go back to order!

So back to the daily routine. Once we tackle some obstacles, we now have to get ourselves dressed and ready to go. My only goal at this time was to look presentable. You know those signs you see on store windows that say No Shirt, No Shoes, No Service? Well, I make sure I follow those rules. I always have a shirt on. It may be filled with leak stains from my lactating breasts because my titty pads moved. It may have a few snacks attached to it because my kid thinks I am a human paper towel. It may even be very wrinkled and have a wet spot because I missed my ironing window and I missed my mouth when I was drinking my Starbucks with a kid attached to my damn arm. I always wear pants because who does that? My pants may have holes from falling several times running after toddlers. They may be too small, and my gut is hanging over because I have ZERO time for the gym, and I eat whatever is available whenever peace and quiet is available. They may be faded because they are old as dirt and the last time I was able to go shopping for myself was PK and now we are three kids deep! Shoes are a must. Most of my shoes are now sneakers, flip-flops or house shoes. This is because they are all the easiest to get on and off and sometimes, I may need to throw a shoe to gain attention to a task or to prevent someone from running into something and ending up with a coconut on their forehead. So, they serve as a distraction to avoid a trip to urgent care. So, to make a long story short, we always have a shirt and shoes, so we always get service!

Have you ever walked out of the house with no bra on hoping that on your quick run to the store you DO NOT SEE ANYONE you know from school, work or play group? I mean, it is six p.m. and you no longer have on your "work" clothes, you took that shit off the moment you got home. You now have on your "mom" clothes. Bra is off and titties are free to roam. It is so liberating, right? So, you forgot that one thing you needed for dinner or you need to pick up more laundry detergent—shit I don't care what it is, but you need it right now. What sucks is that you make it out of your house, out of your driveway, into the store parking lot and into the store without being seen by anyone. You get what you need and haul ass to the counter in five minutes or less and all of a sudden you hear, "Hey Girl! Is that you, Leslie?" You know you have to turn around because your mama taught you better than that and you have manners. You turn around and to your surprise-not really surprised, because you knew the voice when you heard it-you find yourself braless, dirty and with a messy-ass top knot, in front of that one mom from school who never leaves the house without a full set of lashes, make-up, dressed, pressed and ready to impress.

First off, who has three kids under ten and they still have time for a full set of lashes and make-up? Not me! Also, who is still in their "work" clothes after work hours? Not me! Who has help at home to deal with your bad-ass nerve-wrecking kids? Not me! So, once you analyze all that in your head and give her the "once-over look," you say "Hey Girl! What are you doing here?" Which is a dumb-ass question because you clearly see she has a shopping cart full of groceries, so you know why she is here. This question causes her to ask you why you are here all the while she is eye-judging your entire look. But because you are the BAD-ASS MOM you are, just trying to #SURVIVE, you give two fucks and say, "Girl, I was just picking up a few things and heading back home to cook dinner and deal with all my kids!" You exchange a few words about school and homework and upcoming birthday parties, and you are wondering why in the hell of all days, is this line the fucking slowest? Oh wait, I know, because I panicked, I got into the regular line and not the 10 and under hence that is why she is behind me still talking and I'm barely listening. OMG! You get through the line, and say, "OK, nice seeing you and talk to you later!" Haul ass to your truck and go home to kick your flip-flops off and get into your dinner routine!

Let's touch upon those days when you get uninvited guests. I am talking about the ones who come over unannounced, no call and just show up; or the ones your husband invited over and didn't tell you. I am usually a carefree person and love company, but when you are in the AK stage of life, just showing up at a home that houses babies and toddlers and a tired-ass mom, isn't what you want. It's a whole mood. Hair ain't done. Nails look a damn mess and your clothes STANK and don't match at all. You are bleeding 24/7 from your recent delivery of a human from your lady parts, or you have very large breast filled with milk that can't be pumped because they are engorged, and you have a damn fever and everything fucking hurts all the time. Let's not forget when you can't walk to even open the door because you are still healing from your C-section that wasn't planned! I mean to come over to a new mom, old mom or any mom's house uninvited is so rude and inappropriate and I refuse to coddle anyone who gets their feelings hurt.

You know that saying, don't come for me unless I send for you? That applies here, don't come over my house unless I, Me, The Mom, the hourly caregiver, the cook, the cleaner, the judge and jury, send for you. Do not ask me if I want company because if I wanted company, I would call you to say, "Hey, come over!" I didn't call you, so why are you here? WHY? If my husband invited you, did you even think to ask him if I was OK with it? Did you ask him anything about my state of mind? I still feel like a whale. I look like a homeless person in my own house and to top that off, my house is only what I call "mom clean," which means it is clean enough for me and only me at this point in time. I don't have much more to say about this, but I am sure that I am not the only mom who felt this way and still feels this way some days and my kids are older now! Sometimes I wonder did he, my husband, even think that today was NOT the fucking day to tell people to come over? Did he use his memory and remind himself that I was mad this morning, I was mad this afternoon when he called to ask me why I made him another wrap for lunch and I was pissed when he called to tell me he was going to happy hour. Obviously, that didn't cross his mind, so now I have to really be a Bitch and show my ass and also convince his friends to believe that I am crazy and to NEVER EVER just drop by my house without running that shit past me!

I write all of this to get to this one point. Being a mom, new or old, is exhausting, it is challenging, and it really can make you wonder why you chose to keep having kids! The one thing you can always count on when being a mom is that your feelings are ALWAYS valid. They are what keep you #SURVIVIN'. They are what validates you as a mom. Feeling sad, mad, angry, happy, crazy and maybe even irrational on days is OK and totally normal. Pre-Kids, life was easy. After Kids, life will be different, it will be challenging, but most of all it will be so rewarding. So, take each day and make it better than the day before. If you don't have a meltdown on Tuesday but you had one on Monday, Girl you are making moves in the right direction. If you go off on someone you just said a friendly hello to at drop off, and you feel justified in your POP-off, Girl, you are making moves in the right direction! If you somehow get all of your kids to sleep 10 minutes early one day out of the week, GIRL, you are #SURVIVIN' and I am here for all of it!

SURVIVIN' PLAYDATES

THE BEAUTY OF HAVING TWINS IS THAT THEY HAVE A built-in playmate at all times until a certain age. I will not say I do not like playdates at this current era we are in, but they once were one of my favorite things to do. With my oldest, I loved setting up playdates. They were just that, playdates. The girls would laugh, cry, laugh, play, laugh, eat, laugh, play and us moms would sit, talk, get up to stop crying, sit, talk, get snacks for the kids, sit, talk, wipe runny noses, clean hands, sit, talk...you get the idea, right? Setting up a playdate was so easy back in the early 2000s. A simple phone call or face-to-face discussion was all it took to set it up. A park or a house was the usual place of the date. We would bring snacks for our kids only and enough baby wipes to clean a basketball team of kids. Things were so easy. Things were calm. Playdates were my jam. My baby was happy and so was I because after the playdate that meant nap time for at least two hours. It was mommy bliss. I am not sure where things went wrong or who changed the rules of a playdate. The memo was never received, and I never was informed about a meeting to discuss changes to the system that was working and had been working for several decades. Who approved this change? Who thought it was a good idea to change things up on a mama without proper notice? That is breaking mommy code 101, which is don't change shit you didn't start or contribute to its current status of operation. It is not that easy anymore; it is so complicated, and I am so glad I #SURVIVED the new era playdate age because I was very close to being banned from the playdate group text.

When my twins started enjoying playdates or shall I say requesting them, they were already in kindergarten. Some of you may think that is late for playdate season, but I had the beauty of having my wonderful mother-in-law be their sole caretaker from birth to age five. Since they were twins, they had a daily playmate and they never complained. I could take them to the park, and they would have so much fun playing with each other like they just met. They would play outside in the backyard without incident. I never had to ask another mom what her kid's favorite snack was. I never had to request an allergy list and what things their kid was banned from having. I never had to discuss drop-off locations and pick up times. I mean it was easy breezy. Twins were the best for things like this until they got to school, and a mom asked me if my kids could have a play date with her kids.

New-age playdates have so many rules that I got to a point where I could not keep up and just would say "fuck it," if they get mad at my snacks then they don't have to eat them. I ain't got time for this. Whatever is in my pantry is what I'm bringing, and I know my kids will eat it because that is why I have it, because they love that shit!" Did you guys know that you have to bring snacks for the entire playdate group? I was not planning on bringing snacks for more than my two kids. I usually do bring extra but not to share amongst the group. The extras are for when one of my kids spill or drop their initial portion, back-ups are a necessity and the key to not having a tantrum at the park.

When I was asked if my snack was gluten, peanut, cholesterol, diabetes and heart-failure free, I politely—with a slight 'tude in my voice—said, "Uuumm No, I don't believe so, I didn't see that on the package and honestly I wasn't looking. I just grabbed what my kids said they wanted. I'm sorry, did you forget a snack? They can definitely have some of ours!"

The response I got was not appropriate or called for but maybe I deserved it because obviously my ass wasn't keeping up with the playdate logistics. Her response: "Well, if you don't know what's in the box, why are you allowing your kids to eat it? Haven't you heard of a peanut or gluten allergy? Did you even read the text message I sent an hour ago?"

My response: "OK, let me answer all of your questions in the order they were received.

1. My kids are eating them because they like them and that's what I have for today!

2. Yes, I have heard of those allergies, lady, but my kids don't have the allergy so why am I buying snacks based on something they don't have?

3. No I didn't read your text you sent an hour ago in detail because for one it was long as hell and for two I don't care, I'm just here so I don't get fined by my kids, which means I'm just trying to avoid a tantrum today. So, let's deal with this issue right now so we don't have to address it again, I have two kids and some snacks and about two hours to spare. If you don't like my snacks don't eat them, and if you don't like my kids, then stop inviting them to playdates. I came to watch them play, get dirty and possibly cry for a few moments and get over it and then leave to go home and finish the day!"

Her response: "Well, I have my own snacks because my kid has an allergy so...." Then she proceeds to stare at me as I stare at her and the kids at this point are playing. I say "OK," and walk towards the picnic table to sit my tired ass down. This playdate can't get over quick enough and note to self, we ain't doing these ever again. I'm ignoring all requests, you two have a built in, we are good with that! Remember moms, you do what's best for you; it's not your job to manage your own kids' issues and needs along with every other kid in the class. Don't think that you have to brings snacks to please everyone other than your babies to #SURVIVE. You are #SURVIVIN' by just showing up to the playdate, because without that two-hour block of uninterrupted play, you will not make it through your day and that is no way to #SURVIVE!

SURVIVIN' TANTRUMS

I PERSONALLY WAS BLINDED BY THIS STAGE AT FIRST glance with baby number one, because I felt like I was in control of my destiny as being a mommy and no baby would ever embarrass me like I have seen or heard about. I felt like I had the best baby ever when I was around the other moms at the playground or preschool pick-up. I never really understood why they were always in a bad mood or ready for school to start and trying to get congress to lower the age to start kindergarten, to no matter when their birthday fell that year! My first baby had me so blinded, that it wasn't until I had the twinadoes that I realized I had no idea and I definitely needed to take back everything I said about my mommy friends because I now feel and understand their pain. Everything is easy with the first baby(s). You are new to it all and have no idea. You were only told the good stuff, not the shit that really matters. Shame on our mama elders, AKA, mothers, aunts and grandmothers, for not giving us the #MOMTRUTH nothing but the #MOMTRUTH, so help you God. Were you ever told by your mom that you will get yourself ten times over with at least one of your kids? Well, I have, but she seemed to leave out the details and left everything to my imagination. So how am I supposed to know I was a terror when all I hear you tell your girlfriends and co-workers that I am such a great kid and you very rarely had problems with me. That is a pure set-up and not cool mom, not cool!

At four years old, they understand that if you eat what I put on your tray, you get a snack. They believe the dog is a horse and are able to jump on their back whenever they choose. They also know that when Nana, Mimi, Grammie or whatever they call their G-Ma, comes by, they just flash the dimples, widen the eyes and the world is theirs. They will not hear No, EVER! They don't have to eat what's on their plate, they get to eat whatever they want. They understand that if we are in a public place and they really really want something, they only have to cause a scene, which includes having a tantrum, crying that includes big-ass alligator tears, screaming NO really loud in the store or just repeating the word "mommy" over and over again until we give in and give them whatever it is that they want just to shut the hell up. This, my mommy friends, is what we call having a tantrum or a meltdown. I have personally never called them meltdowns because I believe that when something melts it is never getting back to its original state, but when you have a tantrum, once you get that look, that one very specific look, accompanied with some very encouraging words and actions, you will revert back to your original state. But to each its own, Potato, Potato.

Tantrums, meltdown, moments of insanity, minutes of ear-piercing screaming, whatever you want to call it, are the WORST! I mean the WORST! They have literally made me lose my mind and all my religion in public and private, mostly public, but who's monitoring. So, by years three and four, our children may or may not have been brainwashed to behave in a manner that makes us rethink and possibly deeply consider our entire future from behind the bars and gates. Those beautiful eyes and deep dimples get us every time. We buckle and give in and have endless open-ended threats. We laugh at ourselves most days, because we know what we say will never be carried out, but for some reason it feels like a WIN in the books. We are merely learning to #SURVIVE in this space called parenting. Those kids know exactly what they are doing. They are so smart, and anyone who thinks that they have no idea what they are doing, go kick rocks with open-toed shoes on in the desert with no water. I mean it, "Ain't nobody got time for that." The days are long, and the nights are longer. The "I want it" stage has begun and it's a rough one!

Let's break down exactly how they do it to us. First off, let's go ahead and stop beating around the bush and call a spade a spade. What these kids have stumbled upon is the dreaded method of how to throw the forbidden TANTRUM and/or MELTDOWN. I have studied this method for many, many years, my friends. I have gone through three children, two at one time, mind you, who have lost their damn minds and decided that falling their ass to the ground in public is the right way to play the game. So, for those of you who may not know what a tantrum/meltdown is, let me explain. The definition of a tantrum/meltdown is when a small being decides that they are not really accepting your answer of NO to any request, gestures, words, movements, or whatever, so they lose all of their balance and coordination, and fall straight to the floor and immediately their feet start kicking, their arms start flying, their mouths open and nothing, I mean nothing, but high-pitched sounds are coming out and it is very unintelligible. This, my friends, is what we call a TANTRUM, and it only gets worse the longer it goes on. I have a headache just writing about it. I don't know too many moms who can say their kids have not had one, even if it was small, but not one, TANTRUM between the ages of three and five. I'm going to tell you now, I DO NOT BELIEVE YOU. You may be fooling your friends who don't have kids yet or the ones who don't spend all day with their kids, no judgement, I wish that was me some days, but to those moms who are living this stage during this crucial set of years, we don't buy it and we never will.

So, let's talk about how they execute this thing called a tantrum. During the screaming, wailing, crying (not real tears in the beginning) and the stomping, yes some of them will stomp like they pay bills and shit, they fall straight to the ground like they have been shot by a pellet gun in the gut and start wailing and kicking and punching at thin air. I have no idea how they have the lung capacity and cardio skills to keep this shit up for five to ten minutes, but their little asses dig deep and commit to this shit like they are playing their numbers at the slot machine. At times it may seem like they should give up, but they always seem to find a sliver of weakness in their prey, and they re-energize and that scream gets louder and louder by the millisecond. Remember when I said they are crying but the tears are not real at the beginning? Well, they start crying with their eyes closed shut and their mouths wide open, ready for a damn fly to swoop in, and they have ZERO fucking tears falling. But for some odd reason, they have so much snot running from their nostrils to their upper lip, that at this point, you are getting sucked in with no exit strategy in sight. You are getting sucked in because you first wonder how this kid is able to execute this shit with precision and timing, and you then start to feel bad for the people in the public place having to be interrupted by your screaming child as they shop, eat, walk or frankly just breathe. You then start to wonder, how and hell do they have massive amounts of snot falling with no water works? Don't snot and tears work hand in hand? I have never cried without snot, but for some fucking reason, these kids do.

Next, they start yelling your name "Mommy, Mommy, Mommy..." over and over and over again. Shit, we get it, we are mommy, and you want everyone around to know that I am the one is responsible for this atrocious behavior. Thank you, kid! Thank you! I owe you one. So, when you don't answer the first seventeen "mommy's", they get louder and louder each time they say it. They are literally screaming your name across the fucking grocery store like they are on a full-out football field and you are in the nosebleed section. Yeah, it's loud, annoying and its shameful and so fucking embarrassing. So, you do your best to cut a smile and not a frown and walk over or kneel down to try and assist them with getting up, because you want to make it look like they may have tripped or they lost their balance holding onto the cart/buggy. You are trying to indiscreetly show them that they somehow forget that you gave them life and can immediately take it away. As you are performing this small act of kindness, I like to call it, somehow your face makes contact with their finger, fingers, hand or hands, foot or feet, and you forgot you know Jesus and all that he has done for you, and you immediately, for a quick second, I mean quick second, forget that this is your kid, your DNA, your offspring, and you almost defend yourself, because Mama didn't raise no punk and you was always taught, if someone hits you first, you have the right to hit them back. You immediately—remember I said this reaction only lasted for a millisecond, tell yourself it was an accident and a "slip of the finger" like people say they had a "slip of the tongue"—you proceed to get them off the ground with care and tact. You deliver that death stare, that underarm pinch, that back of the neck pinch or that back of the shoulder pinch, and they realize the devil has invaded your eyes and tantrum time is now over.

Some may continue to try your inner gangster, but most know "that look" and what it means, regardless if it is the first time they have seen it or the fiftieth time. When you know, you just know. We all know when mama isn't playing, and game time is over, and she is ready and down for whatever. If you don't know, then I have to say, I feel for you, it's what made me strong and the bad-ass I am today. You then snap back into reality when you hear that word being continually yelled in close proximity to your good ear, "mommy…" so you politely ask your child to get up and get in the cart so you can go and get that toy, snack, game or whatever the fuck it is that they want that caused the tantrum in the first place. This is all a ruse; use it to your advantage. I repeat, you will not give in and give them what they lost their goddamn mind for in a public place, which caused you to sweat, curse, sweat, scream, sweat and did I say curse, in front of innocent bystanders and customers. They will not get that shit, but you really do need them to get up off the floor so you can go along your merry way with whatever you were doing before they decided to act a fool. Two can play that game, and Mommy always does it better.

Once they hear those magic words they have been waiting for, they jump up and lick those boogers and act like they were not just in full- blown straitjacket mode. Most sane people would get Baker Acted for acting like that in public, but not our children. They get a smile and a damn cookie at the least. Well, from my experience, I was bamboozled—I will not lie—but I learned from those encounters and I am now prepared to stand up to my child-size terror. The key to #SURVIVIN' these tantrums/meltdowns is to show your kids that you cannot only act like them, but you can make them start running to fire stations in bunches, to help with looking for a replacement mommy. I have shown my kids my own crazy and they were not only terrified, but they were "shook." They realized that when mommy loses her shit, she really loses her shit and it's not nice. Let me be clear, I am not the one to piss off, offspring or not. DO NOT, I repeat, DO NOT, try my crazy. You will not know what hit you! Also, once you lose your shit on the oldest child, they are pretty good at letting the ones behind them understand what happens to mommy when you really make her mad. They only tell them because their PTSD is in remission and they do not want to mess up a good thing at this point in their life.

They flash us a small innocent smile and open their eyes really wide and just stare at us while smiling, which in most cases may have bought them an extra life. They have no fear at this point what will happen when we no longer fall for their looks. We start to question everything. Like does this get any worse, or will it be over soon? Will they ever sleep in their own bed? Will she ever stop crying? Can I just have one hour of peace—shit, I'll take fifteen minutes at this point? Between three and four years old, they can ask us for what they want, and they understand what NO means, because we say it at least a thousand times a day and it's to the point where when we do say it, it is very rarely said with a smile. At this age, they know that naptime is happening and non-negotiable. This stage is better than the terrible twos. They have more good days than bad days. They are way more fun at three and four than at two. They seem to cry less, but they are learning how to whine. We have a better time with playdates because they just want to run around and have fun. They hug, and pick boogers and will run up to you and give you endless kisses, as long as you have a snack in your hand. Three to four was one of my favorite stages as a mommy with my babies.

Just so you know, if your kid or kids have had a tantrum in public and it was embarrassing, because most of them are shameful, you should never feel like you are a bad parent, never feel like you don't know what you are doing and don't assume that just because your kid/kids are having tantrums and your friends kid/kids are not because they swear that their kids know better, #SURVIVIN' moms will always have your back because we know how it is to be a mom in these kid streets. It's rough, but trust me when I say this, YOU WILL MAKE IT!! I did and wouldn't change a thing about how it all went down. Made my kids stronger, literally—they can do the death drop with no problem—and it made me stronger, mentally, physically (that dead weight of a three-year-old is no joke) and emotionally. Remember you are in control, even if for a moment or two it feels like your mini-me is running the show. It is perfectly OK and acceptable to take a moment to breathe, reflect and regenerate your strength as a BAD-ASS Mom who is just #SUR-VIVIN' and doing a damn good job at it. You Got This, mama, keep pushing and never give up. They will get tired and you will WIN!

SURVIVIN' BACK TO SCHOOL

THE MONTH OF AUGUST IS ONE OF MY FAVORITE MONTHS of the year from the first day until the last day! Why? Are you seriously asking WHY? You must not have any children, or maybe it's that you don't have "happy-place grabbers," I mean precious gifts from God who have turned age five or older by September first. It's the most wonderful time of the year, even better than Our Joyous Holiday Season! When August first hits, I seem to be less stressed, I don't wake up in a bad mood and I actually smile while waking my kids up and making breakfast. All because I know that in a few short weeks, they will be off to a wonderful place called School. I don't care if it's elementary, middle or high, it's all the same. They leave me alone for at least six hours and return with other things to do besides bother the hell out of me! I mean, if you are a stay-at-home Mom, I'm sure you get great pleasure from back-to-school time. If you are a working mom, you get the same pleasure, it's just wrapped a little differently. I look at my kids and say, I dare you to complain, suck your teeth, roll your eyes or just simply ignore me when I wake you up for school.

Mommy wishes she could stay home and have people make her breakfast, lunch and dinner and then say I don't want it. Mommy wishes she could just tell her boss that she just doesn't feel like going in today! Mommy wishes that her clothes, lunch bag and matching accessories were all laid out and ready for her to just put on with little to no work at all! Oh, but mommy can't, my dear child. Mommy has to get her ass up and do all of this shit for you and your siblings, all while listening to you complain about how you don't want to wear a skirt today or you don't like this green polo, but it looks EXACTLY like the other ten you have in your closet. Or maybe you just don't want to eat the beautiful wrap with perfectly sliced carrots and lettuce and EXPENSIVE- ASS deli meat and cheese for lunch because you forgot it's Pizza Day in the cafeteria! Oh, mommy wishes she could just go back to being a damn child and a student! But NO, mommy's ass has to act like an ADULT today and you will respect her while she does it, OK? OK!!

So, let's get a little more real about how we really feel about going back to school! So, the first two weeks of August are like an appetizer that nobody really likes or dislikes, they are a little bland but edible, leading up to that first day of school. These two weeks have days that make me want to lose my mind. They are not really bad days, but I do look at my kids and mouth to them curse words and most times they are not mouthed, they are in the version of an all-out SCREAM! Sometimes I want to actually walk away from my kids in a crowded place and secretly hope they don't come looking for me, but because deep down inside all of my current dislike for those little people who genetically belong to me, I actually would miss them and will kill the first person who lays a fucking breath on my babies without my permission.

These first weeks consist of obtaining the school supply list, gathering all of your online and in-store department store coupons and deciding how many polos and bottoms from last school year still fit. It doesn't sound all bad, I know but also during this beginning week your kids start to ask you annoying questions about back to school, like they haven't been going for the last three years and already know your routine. I mean, if mommy always says no, what makes you think this year will be any different? Questions like, "Mom, can I get three pairs of school shoes?" Uuuummmmmm, no! You will get two pairs like you do each year and you already know I'm not spending over sixty dollars for shoes you will have looking like you've had them for three years in about three days. "Mom, do I have to wear a uniform this year?" Uummmmmmm, yes! Why would you ask me that? Your school has always required uniforms each year and it will never change. Thank the Good Lord! "Mom, can we be on time for School the first day?" Ummmmmmmm, seriously, why is that even a question? Everyone is late the first day, that's totally normal and for the record, 8:34 a.m. is NOT late. It's up to you to get to your first class by 8:35 a.m. If I'm dropping you off before that, it's not my responsibility, you're a middle schooler now. Figure it out, buddy! Love you, have a great day! See you at 3:05. (Insert BIG-ASS SMILE!!!)

The next two weeks of August have lots of good days. Summer is almost over! School is on the horizon and bedtime gets earlier and earlier. Then it starts, "Mom, when are we going school shopping?" It sounds so innocent when you read it, but you know that when it comes out of that small space on their face, you want to punch them. Anyways, so you have to say with a smile or shall I say, little to no attitude or annoyance can be detected in your voice kind of way, "baby, we will go soon." You will then hear, "But when, Mom? Why can't we go today? School is almost here and I want to pick out my own stuff, I'm the one who has to go to school!" Hold the phone, what do you mean pick out your stuff? You don't pick out shit. It's already done for you. That's what a school supply list is for, prepared by your damn school and teachers. The district already said mandatory uniforms about fifteen years ago and the colors are again, chosen by your school and relayed to me, in an email that reads, "Welcome to the 2019–2020 school year! We look forward to a great year of learning with your child and their classmates…blah blah blah…and then at the bottom it reads…in **BOLD**…*uniforms are mandatory, and our preferred colors are blah blah blah!*" So baby, you don't get to pick out a damn thing. Take several seats and we will go when I'm ready! Besides, I already ordered that shit online at Old Navy and the Gap, with a combination of saved gift cards from several returns this summer, endless discount codes found online, and they will be here tomorrow, SUCKAS!!!

Well if you are anything like me, I wait until the last possible minute to take them, not because I'm a procrastinator, but it just gives me some joy to see them frustrated for something they have ZERO control over! I feel empowered for a few days! It is so worth it! Well that is until they decide to be little snitches and tell daddy on me. "Daddy, do you know when mommy plans to take us school shopping?!" So, daddy says to mommy, "Babe, you haven't started school shopping yet? It's like three weeks before school and you have lots to get and you may find yourself running all over town trying to pull it all together." I look at my husband and say, "Oh don't worry, I'm actually taking them today!" Do you think I'm ready to take them today? Hell no, I am still deciding who has the best selection and prices for supplies and shoes, and how many reward points or how much rewards cash can I use towards this purchase. Who has free shipping to the store?

I'm still planning my shopping excursion because I like to save as much money as possible. Back-to-school time is not fair to parents, prices go up and shit is always limited in stores and only three or four registers are open when the fucking store is filled to capacity and kids are throwing shit at each other and running through the aisle while I'm trying to go by my prepared list of shit that never really gets used! I actually would prefer to go alone and at bedtime, so no one says, "Mommy, where are you going? Can I go with you?" In my head I scream HELL NO, take your ass to bed, school starts in three weeks, you need to practice going to bed early and waking up when I scream "get up" the first time. But I refrain from my "I'm about to lose my shit voice" and in the most quiet and polite way say, "Baby, I am going to the store, mommy needs to pick up stuff for breakfast in the morning, OK?" And to answer the second question, I just smile and walk over to my not-asleep-ass child and say, "No, sweetheart, I have to leave right now because Publix is going to close in like ten minutes and you don't want mommy to be left outside, right? So, I have to leave right now and can't wait for you to get dressed, but Mommy will have your favorite foods ready for breakfast tomorrow, OK? Now go to sleep and I will see you in the morning!" Kiss said child on the head and slowly walk-run to the door and do not look back or that's your ass, Mrs. Postman! If you look back, they will come! Don't look back, just leave, I say, LEAVE and move with swift care and tact! Wait, it just hit me while writing this part because I just realized that even though my youngest are thirteen years old, I still have to do this shit just to leave the house and get my shit done in PEACE!! Wow! OK, I'm back…Not really. THEY ARE thirteen and I still have to sneak out of the house! See what I mean about #SURVIVIN'? If you really don't do any of this shit yet, then (1) you must not have any kids, (2) your kids are clones of an unknown species that never do anything to annoy their mom or (3) you are in DENIAL!

So that most favorite Sunday night has finally come. The day before the FIRST DAY OF THE NEW SCHOOL YEAR! You run down your mental checklist that includes, but is not limited to: all kids have bathed, clothes are ironed, book bags are labeled and filled with the unnecessary supplies taken from the list as requested, lunch boxes are in the fridge, breakfast menu is ready and semi-prepared, alarm clocks are set, wine cooler is stocked and ready for action, kitchen is cleaned and laundry room has never been this clean all summer—oh and your keys are chilling on the bar next to your Yeti cup awaiting a fill and retrieval! It's a great night, everyone goes to bed without incident, no one talks back, everyone is excited about the morning! The first day of school is less than twelve hours away!!!! O….M…. G!!!! You made it! They survived! You are not in jail, and your husband is doing what husbands do, just letting you do your thing and out of your way. If he's anything like my husband, he is sitting on the couch watching Sunday Night Preseason Football, ESPN, or preparing for his weekend fishing escapades because he knows what's up.

So, all the kids are in bed, you make sure everything is completely done, no detail has been missed, all the boxes in your mental checklist have been checked. You decide to make it an early night, because you also know that even though you busted your ass tonight, you have to get up super-early tomorrow morning to not only make an amazing First Day of School Kick-Ass breakfast, but you also have to go to WORK!! Well, that all sounded amazing, right? All has been completed and finished, your pillow and bed are calling your name and then it starts…. "Mommy! Mommy! Mom! Mom! Can you please come in my room; I can't sleep!" So, you politely act like you don't hear that voice, one you obviously know very well and know from exactly which direction and room it is coming from, continue on to your room for peace, quiet and possibly some quick adult fun. It keeps getting louder and louder and more high-pitched as you move your feet faster and faster. F-U-C-K!!! Why can't they just go to sleep all ready? School starts in less than ten hours and you seem to not be able to GO THE HELL TO SLEEP!! So, you do what all of us moms do, you go and see what is wrong. "Hey baby, what's wrong?"

"Mommy, I can't sleep, I am too excited for tomorrow and I'm scared."

OK, let's stop for a quick minute and analyze this statement in our heads before we comfort our child tonight. So, you are saying you are excited and scared at the same damn time? So, what has you so excited that it is scaring you too? Are you excited to meet your new teacher? OK, I understand that, but if you don't go to sleep you can't meet them at all because you will oversleep and miss the entire first day. So, you should only be scared if you are going into what we consider a milestone grade, Kinder, sixth and ninth? Let's be real, Moms, #MOMTRUTH time, we all know that those other grades are cute, but we really don't put as much energy into them as we do the MILESTONE grades. I mean Kinder starts off the whole educational game. Fifth grade is ending the elementary experience. Sixth grade means you are entering Middle School and teenage years are upon us. Ninth grade is that grade that says to us parents, these next four years are all I have left to brainwash them. It goes by so quickly, those last four years, I couldn't believe it. OK, back to the lecture at hand, so what exactly are you scared of? You have been going to the same school with basically the same kids for at least three years now, I think we can skip this emotion at this point.

"Sweetie, I know you have many emotions about tomorrow but TRUST Mommy when she says, everything will be perfect tomorrow but only if you close your eyes and let your brain get the much-needed rest it deserves. Your brain will be working so hard tomorrow to remember your new teachers, friends and all of the fun that you will have tomorrow. But if you don't go to sleep RIGHT NOW, you will have a very tired brain and tomorrow will not be fun! And you want to have fun on the first day of school, right?"

"'Yes, mommy!"

"OK, well let's get some sleep so we can be ready for the best day ever!"

"OK, mommy! See you in the morning! Oh, and I don't want to wear a skirt tomorrow, I want to wear my shorts with my pink shirt, not my yellow one, OK mommy? Love you and good night!"

And just like that, you have wasted ten minutes of your "me" time to comfort your kid who in the end only wanted to change up their uniform that has already been coordinated with matching socks and hair accessories OH and let's not forget ironed and on hangers in the closet ready for wear!! At this point, you want to punch them in the face because they obviously don't care about your mental health or physical health at this point. You try your best to squeeze out a smile, because you do not have the time to start a fight at nine p.m. with your ten-year-old, who will start crying and then that will wake up every other kid who is sleeping peacefully in your house and cause you to really lose your shit, which in turn will cause said husband to walk into the inappropriate yelling match you are having with your ten-year-old, and he will ask you why can't she change her mind on what she wants to wear to school, which will lead you to want to punch him the face too, but instead you give him that look that says, YOU just lost your playdate, buddy!

But instead of taking this approach, you just say, "OK, Goodnight and see you in the morning, baby! Say your Prayers, because God loves you!" Your kids know when you have that calm voice and give it over to the Lord, that they are one question away from a fucking curse word, inappropriate name calling, or scene from their mom, and they really don't want to deal with it at this point, so they end all convos that they see going this way, with a "Love you!" At this point, your loving husband did not get involved in any part of that transaction, therefore his playdate is still on for tonight and no longer pending, and you are off to your room to shower and enjoy your night that you have been waiting for all summer!

BRIIIIINNNNNNNNGGGGGGGGGGGGGGGGGG-GGG!!!

That is the sound of your damn alarm going off at 4:40 a.m. (don't judge, those extra ten minutes give me so much life) on a Monday morning, also known as the FIRST DAY OF SCHOOL! You get up and get yourself all the way together. By the time you leave your room and attempt to step in the hallway to awaken the happiness-grabbers, you realize that you have a few minutes to spare to either watch the morning news, troll Facebook or IG, read a few emails, make yourself cup of coffee/tea or wine (we don't judge) or just plain sit in silence. This is because you know it will probably never come again, at least for this week, so take advantage of this rare opportunity when you can. This particular morning you are well rested and ready to tackle the world, and you already anticipate it to include sweet morning wake-ups, which will probably be followed by lots of partial sentences that include the words hell, fuck, damn, let's go, late and NOW. But as us moms do; we keep it moving whether it be through a smile or an all-out scream.

So, you step into the hallway and realize that you hear familiar, but unfamiliar noises. They are coming from behind closed doors that supposedly are where you left your children sleeping in their beds. So you try to make out the sounds which sound like running water, dressers being opened and closed and you also try to make out the unfamiliar and STRONG smells of too much deodorant and toothpaste, Axe or Bath and Body Works body spray being doused into mouths and onto skin. I can say this because my youngest kids are thirteen, so this is that normal middle-school pre-teen first day of school start-up kit. But for those of you who have younger kids, you may still hear noises that include water running, which either means your boys are peeing on the floor yet again, kids are brushing their teeth and washing their face or simply forgot to turn the damn faucet off last night; either way, it means the day is here and has already started without fair warning of good or bad. Remember; this is the first day of school so you continue on with the routine of waking up your children as any good parent would do on the first day of school, and possibly days following, depending on how you are feeling.

You open each door and say, "Good Morning! It is time to get up and get ready for school! Breakfast has started and I will meet you in the kitchen. Let's go, we have to make sure we leave on time today, you don't want to be late, day one!" The response can be either one of two ways. Option 1: "Good morning, Mom! I am brushing my teeth and washing my face. I am going to get dressed soon and I am so excited!" Maybe not verbatim, but something along the lines of, hello, I am up, and I am getting ready, see you in a few minutes. Option 2: "Uuugghhhhhh, I'm still tired! I don't want to get up right now, can I sleep for another five minutes? Why are you waking me up so early? Who cares if we are late, everyone is late the first WEEK of school, mom. Please five more minutes, I'm sooooo tired!" Again, the response may not be verbatim, but it's lined up almost perfectly. So, us Moms have to decide how we respond to Option 2, because Option 1 is what we pray for at night and God listened and answered! Option 2 response has to be done with great care and tact so that we can continue on with our regularly scheduled program and also so that the other kids know and understand, DO NOT TRY ME LIKE THIS EVER AGAIN! You know put that fear of MOM (God is what most say) in them for at least the moment, so you can keep your pressure at the recommended minimum.

So your response to Option 2 is initially a repeat of your first "Good morning, wake up," and if that does not go as you want, then you add a little bit of Please don't make me repeat myself again with that "Don't piss me off" look. If that doesn't work, you head to the "are you fucking serious voice" that includes a rendition of something like this: "I have asked you three times to get up and get dressed. I don't have time to keep going back and forth with you this morning. You have asked me for five more minutes and you were granted those requested five minutes. How, you ask? Well the seven minutes you have taken arguing with me about not getting your ass out of bed is two minutes over the requested five. So, get your ass up, get dressed and get downstairs to eat in the next thirty minutes. You will not be late to school today and I WILL NOT be late to work for this shit. I don't want to hear another word from you, and don't forget you have thirty minutes to get downstairs to eat breakfast." You walk out and head into the next rooms for hopefully an easier morning wake-up. If the others were up, they have just realized the tone has been set for the morning. If they are still in bed, because we know they are not sleeping through all of that yelling that just happened, but if they are still in bed, they have jumped their asses out of bed and are in their respective bathrooms to get ready and they too will be downstairs in thirty minutes—shit, more like twenty to twenty-five—because they want to see what happens if their sibling misses the deadline.

You get downstairs to the kitchen to start breakfast. Your husband has either left for work already or getting ready to leave for the day. Some of our husbands will know that just kissing us and saying "Have a great day, Babe" is all we want to hear and will tolerate, but some of us have that husband who will dare to say, "Babe, why all the yelling this morning? It's the first day of school, don't start out in a bad mood or don't put the kids in a negative space today. Its early, everyone is tired." If it is statement number two, you look at his ass with that "I'm so done with your ass today" look and proceed to start breakfast. You purposely move slowly with his breakfast and/or lunch because he has pissed you off and it was uncalled for. You don't come into his place of business and tell him to chill out, and don't put negative energy into the workplace. Everyone is tired today, so you give two middle fingers up about his food intake at this moment. So, hubby leaves for work after several goodbyes and hugs accompanied with kisses and all the positive encouragement, he feels they need because Mommy has not started it off so well. The door politely closes behind him and you then proceed to let your kids know that now that Daddy is gone, get to moving. We have to go! I have to get to work and I am already late.

They proceed to the breakfast table to eat halfway dressed, or they have an attitude because the hair isn't how they want it, or THEY ARE NOT HUNGRY! I can deal with the first two pretty well—You can finish getting dressed downstairs but not at my table. I can do my best to fix your hair and we can make moves for a better hair day tomorrow. BUT when they complain about that FINE breakfast that you slaved over this morning at 5:45 a.m., that shit will make you reevaluate your entire life from that point on. You immediately change up your first day of school mom face to the What the Fuck did you just say to me? Mom face. I know I hear shit different sometimes, I may have misunderstood you because maybe you were yawning when you said it or maybe you were mumbling, but please repeat what you just said. And just like that, they repeat it with clarity and sass, I DO NOT WANT TO EAT BREAKFAST!!! Wait a minute little kid, those are fighting words. I have told your ass before to not try my inner gangsta. I'm boujie but I am definitely from these streets and I will fight you. Seriously, let me explain myself to you and all that I have been through to get to this point in my life this beautiful Monday morning, that the Lord has made, and let ME rejoice and be glad in it. Also let's analyze the details together for one quick moment of your time, not my time, because today is all about you, NOT ME, and maybe you will want to redact your statement and follow-up with a new and improved one.

This is you, explaining yourself to your kid, because for some odd reason, we always seem to find ourselves explaining why we do shit and why we say shit to our kids as if we owe them an explanation for their troubles of listening. I do not recall my mom ever explaining herself to me or my brother. She would just say, insert the NeNe Leakes voice, "I said what I said!" and we never said another word, made another comment or asked another question. Now let me be clear, I do not explain the details for this analytical moment, because at this point, my blood pressure is sky high, my clothes are discombobulated on my body, my hair has fallen and my face is hot because I was trying to be EXTRA and figured today called for a fresh face day, and since I never buy myself anything fancy anymore these days, I scoured my house and I used that new Fenty Beauty make-up I found in one of MY bathrooms, which I realized later was my older daughter's collection. Why did I use her stuff without asking, you may ask? For one, I PAID for that shit and for two, it's in my house where she uses everything without asking first, like water, electricity, cell phone towers, cell phone, cable, internet, should I keep going. NO. OK, and in case you missed it the first time I said it, I PAID for that shit. She has no job, pays no bills and I can use what I want, when I want. Proceeds with the explanation with attitude and slightly aggressive body movements, that are unpredictable at this moment.

So, just so you know, my ass used all my battery life on my iPhone X, along with my mophie and my portable charger, because all yesterday, while I was prepping your shit for your first day of school today, I was stalking mom blogs, mom sites, Pinterest, YouTube, IG and Facebook, just so that I could find the PERFECT breakfast of champions for my beautiful babies. In between, cooking dinner for your asses last night, ironing your uniforms, labeling your school supplies and organizing your backpack, oh and making you a bomb-ass gourmet lunch, that your friends will be like, "OOOOHH-HHWEEEEE...Your mom made you the best lunchbox ever, can we swap?" You will be like "OOOOOHHHHWEEEEE, Naw, I'm good." I also managed to go to Publix, Costco, Trader Joes and Whole Foods all within a three-hour time slot avoiding the back to school rush, going over three—yes, three—different grocery lists, because I researched all morning, before the fucking sun was up, as to what store had what and who had the better prices and important shit like that us mom's look for in a grocery store. I also made sure everything was nut free, gluten free, low sugar, low carbs, low fat, fuck low everything but high in energy and healthy shit. I worked my ass off to make this meal for you, but no, you have decided to let me know that you do NOT WANT your beautiful gourmet breakfast of champions or you do NOT LIKE your gourmet breakfast of champions and you would rather eat breakfast at school or better yet, have the audacity to ask me if I will stop at McDonald's or Starbucks and get you all something to eat.

So now I you have explained myself and laid out all of the very important details to this beautifully, well-planned, well-plated and well-balanced breakfast of champions meal, are you ready to redact, recall, restate, rephrase, re-something, before I go postal all up and through this kitchen? So, you believe in your heart, body and mind that they will say, "I'm sorry, mom. I would love to eat this beautifully balanced and perfectly plated breakfast of champions meal. I am so grateful to have you in my life and to care about my dietary needs with such passion and commitment." Or something along those lines. But instead, they look you square in your eyes they do not blink, breathe or move a muscle and say with fucking ATTITUDE, OK, BUT I DID NOT ASK YOU TO MAKE ME A FANCY MEAL, I AM NOT HUNGRY RIGHT NOW AND I DO NOT WANT TO EAT.

WHAT THE FUCK DID YOU JUST SAY, LITTLE KID?!! This has to be a joke, right? Ashton Kutcher is going to jump his ass out of my pantry and say I am being punked right now, right?

Have you guys seen or heard of Madea, from the Tyler Perry movies? Well anytime someone has any type of attitude in their heart, mind, spirit, speech or body, she goes all the way in on their asses and that is exactly who we start channeling when we lose our shit that Monday morning. You literally start cursing, yelling, spitting, stomping, and doing whatever else you have to do to let their asses know that they are going to sit their asses down right now and eat every fucking drop of food on that beautifully plated dish and drink that entire glass of fresh-pressed orange juice that took you an hour to do and they will wash their breakfast dishes and have their asses at the door by 7:45 a.m. SHARP. Oh— and you remind them if they decided to "tell Daddy on you," they will regret it, and you walk away by giving them the death stare.

Now back in the day, the early stages of first being a mommy, I would go into the bathroom and cry and give myself a pep talk and shit, fix my face and go back out there to stand up to my bullies like nothing happened. I used to think it was only me, but after speaking, well let's just be real and say, crying to my girlfriends about what a bad day, morning, night or week I have had with my kids, I realized quickly, I was not the only one going through it and some of them were handling it worse than me or some couldn't even make it to the bathroom without breaking down in front of their kids. I was learning as they were, but we never stopped to ask each other about what's going on in each other's mom life because we felt embarrassed and ashamed. We were individually #SURVIVIN' when we had a whole tribe to #SURVIVE with. So, this time, wasn't like the first time or even the tenth time, it was the FINAL time, because the way you lost your shit today you are hoping that you will never have to do it like that again. You have been through this too many times already, so Mommy, get your shit together, smile, fix your clothes, put on your heels and finish eating your deliciously plated breakfast along with your fresh pressed orange juice made from organic oranges from Whole Foods, wash your dishes and grab your lunch box, purse, and YETI cup and be ready to leave their asses at home if they are not by the garage door in the next twenty minutes. You #SURVIVED that shit and you are still #SUR-VIVIN'. They will never know that it's a constant struggle to deal with their shit day in and day out and still have the same unwavering love you have had for them since the day when you were blessed to be their mommy!

SURVIVIN' THE DROP-OFF LINE

OK, SO I HAVE A LOT TO LET OUT ON THIS TOPIC. I HAVE no idea where to start. I have talked about random school/kid topics with my best mom/girlfriends for years, and even though we all have very different stories about many topics, the one topic that we all agree on, have similar disgust about, curse the most about, get super annoyed about each and every school year, is the FUCKING DROP-OFF LINE. I mean it is so fucking simple moms, dads, nannies, grandmas, grandpas, and so on. Well, let me backup, it actually must not be that simple to everyone because 99.9% of the people dropping off to school in a vehicle do not seem to understand the concept. So, let me start right in and explain it the best fucking way that I can. Also, a side note, this topic actually does not make me want to curse my kids; it makes me want to—actually I do—curse the other kids' damn parents or whoever the hell is in charge of drop-off.

OK, so let's start with the drive to school. When I FINALLY get my kids in the car and we are on the way to school, we discuss various things. We talk about homework, we talk about lunch, we discuss friends and parties and bullies and all that good stuff. We talk about our weekend, the upcoming weekend, vacations and anything else they want to talk about. Many times, we don't talk, or we don't talk that much. They are reading a book, finishing homework (don't judge me), listening to music, studying or sleeping. Usually when we are about fifteen minutes from school, I let them know how much I love them, I tell them to have a good day, I scold them about an email I just got or I tell them to behave today, because ain't nobody got time for a phone call from the principal, teacher or somebody else's parent about some bullshit. I also make sure to tell them to fix their hair, zip their bookbag, reach in the third row and grab their shit from the seat, grab their jacket/sweater and finally get ready to get out because I have to get to work on time today.

So, we pull up to the long-ass line on the street, waiting to move onto the "Porch" they call it. It is just the circle driveway that leads to the "doorway" of the school. But for some odd reason, these bitches like to call it the "Porch." Wait, let me explain the directions that we receive each and every year, via IG, Twitter, Facebook, email, text alert and automated call from the principal.

"Good evening Parents, and welcome back to the 2019–2020 school year. We are so excited to see each and every one of you tomorrow as we embark on this wonderful school year. I am most delighted to greet each and every one of your children tomorrow morning as they enter into their transformed classrooms to learn, grow and enjoy their teachers, friends, administration and staff. I also wanted to remind you all of our drop-off and pick-up procedures. These procedures will go into effect on the fourth day of school. But it would be great if we could all start implementing them as of tomorrow. This way it gives our new parents time to get acclimated with the procedures. If you plan to walk your child into the front office hallway, please park your car in a designated area. If you plan to drop your child off, please proceed to the "Porch" and once you arrive on the "Porch" area, your child can get out of the car with their belongings and proceed into the school. Please do not get out of your car or put your car in park. Our goal on the "Porch" is to keep continuous movement so that everyone gets into the school safely and on time. Also, please remember we are a "No Cell Phone while on Porch" school, so please be hands-free or not on the phone during drop-off. If you have any questions, we can address them at "Back to School Night" in a few weeks. Thank you for your time and we wish everyone a wonderful first day back to school!"

That is the voicemail version, and the Twitter, IG Facebook, text and email version is this same script that you will get to via a link or attachment. Basically, it says, you have three days to get your shit together. After that, please drop your kids off either by parking and walking them to the school entrance or dropping them off on the "Porch" and keep it moving. If you need to talk to your kids and have a full fucking conversation with them, Park. If you put their backpacks in the trunk of your car and they can't get them out themselves, Park. If you need to fix their uniform, brush their hair, give them three-thousand kisses on each cheek and say goodbye in five different languages, Park. But if your kids can open the door, say goodbye and get their stuff in under thirty seconds, the "Porch" is for you, my friends. Some of you reading this may be laughing because you totally understand where I am coming from. Some of you may be offended, and if you are, I DO NOT CARE. Some of us have to get to work in a timely fashion. Some of us said our goodbyes at the door before we left the house or right before we got close to the school. Some of us are not in denial about our kids' capabilities. You know if your kid can close the door by themselves or get their backpack out of the trunk by themselves. If you don't know, you'd better ask somebody. Drop-off is nothing to play with, when you have a mom like me behind you in a Suburban glaring at your ass the entire five minutes you are taking to drop your ten-year-old off. Yes, I know they are ten, they are in the same class as my kid. Shit, my kids have been doing drop-off methods since they were in second grade, you gonna learn today baby. You gonna learn today!

I have no idea if you have experienced the amount of anger and frustration I have felt during this process. It has gotten to the point of an all-out fight on the "Porch" because the asshole in front of me has no consideration for my time and that pisses me off. I will record your ass and blast you on social media just to make a point and then maybe you will get the point. One time in particular that sticks in my mind, is when this lady was dropping off her daughter and it took her ten minutes to get her ass off the "Porch." Why, you may ask? Because she had to fix her ponytail while the child was sitting in the back seat, get her jacket from the front seat, get her backpack from the trunk, put the jacket on the eight-year-old girl while she was still sitting in the back seat, fix her bow, because it got tilted from the jacket situation, unbuckle the little girl from the back seat—yep, you read that right, she had to unbuckle her ass—then the little girl got out. After she got out, she had to roll her backpack to her from the backside of the car, go back to the front seat, get her lunch box, walk back to the child standing on the "Porch" right by the door, attach the lunch box to the backpack, zip the jacket up, fix the bow yet again, and then she starts her goodbye process. She gives her a hug, then gives her two kisses, one on each cheek, hugs her again, kisses her again, twice, once on each cheek AGAIN, and then she decides to I will assume, tell her to have a great day, eat all of her lunch, make good choices, enjoy her friends, turn in her homework, do her homework and at least one-hundred other unnecessary things to say at the at the drop-off line on the "Porch," and you have already wasted three-and-a-half minutes of my time. She finally lets the little girl go, ever so slightly, with yet another kiss and a wave. Lady, she is right in front of you, why are you waving?

FUCK, at this point, just put her ass back in the car and take her wherever the hell you are going, because obviously you have separation anxiety. Please, I am begging you, let me go to work. My kids have been out of my car for ten minutes now, because they got out early, even though I have been sitting behind you for ten minutes, my kids don't play around. They want to be there for morning P.E. It is an essential part of their day. Your kid, on the other hand, has no problem with missing the morning session of box ball. Shit, that is the talk of the afternoon at pick-up, who lost in morning P.E. box ball and who won the actual P.E. or recess championship. So anyway, I digress, so the lady is waving, the little girl finally turns around, so no eye contact is being made, and starts to walk to the office hallway. She is almost there and this *&%#* decides to fucking honk her horn and WAVE AGAIN! O...M...G...!! LEAVE, LADY, JUST PUT YOUR FOOT ON THE GAS PEDAL AND DRIVE AWAY!!!! THIS IS TORTURE!! But guess what, the little girl is just as annoyed as I am. She does not turn around, she keeps walking because the Lord heard my prayers, and her little friend walked right up to her and they run off down the hallway out of her mother's fucking sight. I was like, Thank you Jesus! Amen! Hallelujah! Praise the Lord! Now MOVE!!

Well, unfortunately for me, she starts to move and realizes that she never closed her trunk. So, she has to put the car in park, take off her seatbelt, unlock her door, open her door, put one foot at a time on the ground, very slowly at that, push up on the side of the door, to get up out of the seat, get out of the car, close the door, walk S L O W L Y to the back of the car, put her hands on the trunk and pull down, S L O W L Y, press down like five times to make sure it is shut, walk back to the front of the car, but this genius goes the opposite direction. She goes the fucking long way, all the way around the passenger side, and she is walking so slow, I could have walked to the P. E. court, destroyed a few kids in box ball and walked slowly back to my Suburban, turned on my Spotify playlist, run through a few songs and then change the list so I could be in my "commute to work" zone, and she would still not be on the driver's side yet. She finally gets to the driver side, opens the door, S L O W L Y gets in, closes the door very S L O W L Y, turns the key, put her seatbelt on, puts the car in drive and by this time I am laying on my horn with no stopping in site because I am annoyed, hot, pissed, frustrated and cursing so loud they can hear me with the windows up and my Beyoncé playlist blaring. She finally takes her foot off of the brake and starts to go and then what to my fucking surprise, the fucking dad in front of her, is still putting on his son's jacket and having a full conversation about something I don't fucking care about. So, I'm like obviously these people are doing just fine and don't need to actually get to work on time. This shit can't be real. I have never wanted to punch someone in the face so badly as I wanted to this day. I arrived at the "Porch" at 8:01 a.m. I left the "Porch" at 8:28 a.m. School starts in seven minutes; I might as well stay for lunch at this point. PISSED!

So, as you can tell, the drop-off line is my nemesis. I can't stand it. I can't stand the people who hold me up from getting to my place of work. I can't deal with the useless school security, who sees this shit happening in front of them and stands there, because they don't want to miss out on those end-of-year gifts. I have to #SURVIVE the drop-off line every day and it never gets better. The problem is, the ones who hold the line up every day, are the ones who have been doing this process for at least three years now. I have assumed that retention is not their best quality and never has been. This is just my story, but my mom friends have way worse ones than this. But as we always do, we figure out a way to keep #SURVIVIN' these crazy-ass school days. If you can #SURVIVE the drop-off line, trust me, you can #SURVIVE anything. Sometimes people need a good morning curse out. Sometimes people need to see your alter Ego. Sometimes people need to understand your struggle so that they can really understand what #SURVIVIN' with kids really is like. You can just simply tell them, you don't have to go home, but you have to get the Hell off the "Porch" because I have places to be, unlike your ass. Then you put your foot on the gas pedal and go about your merry way totally unbothered and feeling great because you #SURVIVED the drop-off line yet another day.

SURVIVIN' THE PICK-UP LINE

SO, AS WE ALL KNOW, IF YOU ARE DROPPING OFF YOU obviously have to pick up. I mean we don't have to pick up if we really don't feel like it that day, but just be prepared for "those moms" to be your judge and jury and let everyone know at school that you were late picking your baby up. When you finally get there, your child is sitting on the bench rocking back and forth with those big-ass alligator tears, saying "Mommy, why didn't you pick me up from school again?" That immediately pisses you off, because you and that damn kid know that, that one time, you "forgot" to pick them up was not really like that. You were late and the ladies on the "Porch," who hate you, took your child to the office five minutes earlier than the designated time to say a parent is late. This was all because you were trying to do your grocery shopping before pick- up because you got off of work earlier than expected and you remembered that not only did two kids have tutoring tonight, one had volleyball and one had lacrosse and you didn't have time to go on Sunday, because your husband was out of town and you were bombarded with laundry and preparing dinner. So when you were done with all your shit at work, you looked up and noticed, you have a whole forty-five minutes before pick-up line gets crazy, so why not stop at Publix and get a few things to last you until at least Wednesday, when your husband is expected to be back in town. Not that he will help you out, but at least you can call him to go pick a kid up or take them to practice if needed. We all know it sounds good, but it almost never turns out that way. So anyways, the moral to this digression is, pick your kid up on time and don't make enemies, because they will try to destroy you! Trust me, I know.

So, again, if you drop off, you have to pick up! The pick-up line gives some of my mom friends heart palpitations daily and they SHIVER if they are a minute late. I no longer shiver because I have my kids trained after the said incident noted above. Check your phones, iPods, iPads, email or whatever you need to before you say I am late. Ask your teachers if they have an email from me before you walk out of that classroom door. Check every car before you take your ass back in that school saying your mom is not here today. Don't try me. I may be late; that is OK. I may not be in the same spot I was yesterday; that is OK. I may not be picking you up today; that is OK. What is not OK, is you making false accusations on my character. I fight kids and my own kids are not above that rule. But unfortunately, my mom friends get crazy about pick-up lines. I don't think you understand how crazy they get. OK, let me attempt to provide you with enough description so that you can visualize the crazy.

Well, the pick-up line for schools here in Miami is not OK. It has nothing to do with anything else except crazy parents and their crazy after-school commitments. School gets out at 1:50 p.m. daily for Pre-K and Kindergarten, 3:05 p.m. for grades two to five, and if it is a K to eight center, the sixth to eighth graders also get out at 3:05 p.m. Monday, Tuesday, Thursday and Friday. On Wednesdays only, all K-8 Centers and all traditional elementary schools get out at 1:50 p.m. Traditional middle schools get out at 3:50 p.m. and high schools get out at 2:20pm, daily. Most elementary students in Pre-K thru fifth grade are walked outside to their designated spots at 3:05, and they usually are met either by their parents standing on the sidewalk of the "Porch" or the parents are parked in the pick-up line that starts on the "Porch." Middle-school and high school students mostly govern themselves accordingly, but some schools have designated spots for pick-up.

Miami Dade schools are overcrowded and most, if not all, schools are in the middle of residential neighborhoods, so the parking is a joke and the traffic is a nightmare. I mean the amount of double parking that goes on and the hazard lights flashing on and off, is not OK. I mean we all know you are here for pick-up, why are your hazard lights on? We see the school magnet on the back of your trunk, we know you are here for pick-up. We see you every day, we know you are here for pick-up. One of my good friends has told me about a parent who actually has asked other patiently waiting parents, if they can have their spot so the child in the car seat doesn't have to sit in the sun for an hour as they wait. Yep, that happened, true story. I have heard so many more just like it. I always say, it has never happened to me or will never happen to me because I think they see the crazy all over me. I have seen parents squeeze their full-sized SUV—I'm talking about Suburbans, Escalades, Expeditions—into small-ass spots that are probably just enough room for let's say, a Honda or Toyota car—not an SUV! Once they feel that they are in that small-ass spot, all you see is the ass of that Suburban out in the road, because they are too damn lazy to park and walk, or too much of an asshole to get in the back of the line, because they don't feel like waiting today or they can't wait because they have somewhere to be. Oh, and don't get me started on the damn golf carts who think they own the road and will slide their little asses in between shit to get in front of you. YOU ARE NOT DRIVING A CAR, LADY!! THAT IS A DAMN GOLF CART AND THE CLOSEST GOLF COURSE, WELL I DON'T KNOW WHERE THE CLOS- EST ONE IS, BUT IT AIN'T HERE, SO BYE FELICIA!

I have a question for you. Do you think it is necessary to be in your pick-up line an hour to an hour and a half before school is dismissed? Well, my mom friends sure do. I know a few who will drive themselves crazy at work trying to get to that damn pick-up line early so they are either first in line, close to the front of the line, parked near the flagpole for easy visibility of their child when they arrive on the "Porch" with their teacher, and some just get there early because they were crazy enough to make a doctor's appointment for fifteen minutes after the bell rings. I am serious, people, I know and love people like this, but I would not imagine living like this daily to pick my kids up.

So, I have this one mom friend who is super crazy about being the first person to the doctor's office right after dismissal. What this means, for those of you who are confused, is that her Orthodontist is very popular at her school and amongst the community schools in the area where her children attend. So, when her kids have follow-ups at the Ortho, for some crazy and messed-up reason, she thinks that she has to beat everyone else to the office. See, everyone gets out of school at the same time, so everyone who has an appointment after school is headed to the same place she is. The catch is, we all know these Orthos are totally overbooked and have like 400 kids scheduled for six-week checks all at 2:30 p.m. Well school gets out at 1:50, so everyone is rushing there. EVERYONE is RUSHING there for their 2:30 spot. Once you get there, your kid has to sign in and you are called back by the hygienist in the order in which you signed your ass in. So if you get the parking lot first but your kid takes their sweet-ass time walking in, while you park, most likely they will get trampled by three other kids and now instead of being first they will be fourth, fifth, or dare I say sixth. So, my friend thinks it is appropriate to schedule her kids' six-week check-up for 2:00, and again, in case you missed it, school is out at 1:50 p.m. SCHOOL IS OUT AT 1:50 P.M.!! But that shit doesn't even make her sweat. She has her babies trained. So, one day, she has her daughter's check-up scheduled for 2:00p.m. and her baby knows the drill. Let me try to break this crazy shit down for you.

Well, she has her daughter go to the kindergarten "walkers" area so that she can get to the car faster instead of waiting on the "Porch" for her to drive up. The bell rings and she is waiting for her baby to get to the door and RUN, yes, I said RUN, to her. In this area, the parents have to be visible to security because the kids are in the "walkers" area, which means they are walking home alone or with someone. They have a special pass. I have no idea how her ass has a "Porch" pass and a "walker's" pass, because I think you are only allowed one, but if you knew her, you wouldn't even dare to ask how she pulled that shit off, she is a genius. It's amazing to watch her work most days. I digress. Anyway, she is waiting on the sidewalk next to her car and she sees her baby in the window of the door. Her daughter is first to the door, but when she goes to push it open, it won't budge. After a few seconds, yes seconds, I'm talking maybe ten, the panic in her baby's face starts to set in because she knows what is at stake. First in line or fifth in line, and in their house, fifth ain't acceptable. LOL! So after about one minute, my friends spots the custodian trying to get the kids out. Well, it appears the door is broken or the lock is broken, at this point she doesn't care what is what. She locks eyes with her daughter, her daughter locks eyes with her and "POOF" off they go to meet up. Her daughter picks up her rolling fucking backpack and slings it onto her back, takes off and hits a few corners until she gets to the front of the school. My girlfriend hits her outside corners at 20 mph and hauls ass to the front of the school and within five seconds they are REUNITED and off they go. Mom snatches the bookbag clean off her daughter's back, her daughter holds on to her mom's hand and off they run back around the corner hitting those bitches with speed and tenacity, car doors get unlocked, trunk popped, that baby jumps in backseat, mom throws the bookbag in trunk, hits the button, slides down the driver's side of the car and slides into the driver's seat with ease, hits the "IGNITION" button and is the first person on the main street headed north towards the Ortho. This is all happening, all while the FIRST, yes, the FIRST car on the "Porch" is still loading passengers. The clock says 1:55 p.m. as she glides down the street, all within the school zone speed limit. She hangs a right into the parking lot, daughter jumps out, runs into the front door, mom hangs a left and parks, mom walks in smoothly about thirty seconds after her daughter, and at 2:02, I get a text message with a pic attached, that says, "Peace Out Suckaaaaasss!!!" tongue face emoji, tongue face emoji, tongue face emoji, followed by two pics, one of them taking a selfie in the car and the other is the twelve cars turning in for parking as kids are hopping out one by one running to sign in at the front desk. She follows it up with a video of moms yelling at their kids to get out, run faster, hurry up and sign in before anyone else comes, all with them ending in the classic, "Tell them I'm parking" line. OMG, I died of laughter because her baby was cool as a polar bear's toes in the Arctic, all while eating her after-school snack UNBOTHERED. I was like that baby is the REAL MVP! She is only nine and has that shit down packed. My kids would have lost their damn minds.

I tried once to be a daredevil and make an Ortho appointment for fifteen minutes after dismissal and I almost had a nervous breakdown from the anxiety. My kids even thought I was crazy. They thought there was a family emergency because of how frantic I was screaming at people on the road to drive faster, mind you they were driving 10 mph above the speed limit and we had a few school zones to go through. I was a maniac. I couldn't even pull my shit together once I got to the office, and it was even worse when I got home. It was like I had PTSD because I kept replaying the nonsense in my head and getting stressed all over again. I think I even suffered from night terrors and sweats for a few weeks following this ridiculous recommendation from said friend. I refuse to do that shit again, but I know moms who will do that every day and still be frantic, anxious and stressed and then go on about their day when they get to their destination like they didn't just curse out at least 20 people on the road trying to be safe as they make their way to their destination in one piece.

I have asked my mom friends who are crazy about the pick-up line, what do you do for an hour as you wait to pick your kids up? The answers I have received literally have me dying of laughter because they are insane. One has told me that she shops for Christmas presents online in the pick-up line. Lady, it is fucking August, and weren't you home all day before you came here? You couldn't have done that at home? At work? Anywhere but here, right? You must have unlimited data because the Wi-Fi signal from the school sucks. Another mom friend has told me that she scrolls through social media for that hour. I am like OK, I am a sucker for scrolling and slightly stalking people on IG too, but for an entire hour? Don't you get bored? Who are you stalking, lady? Do we need to get the authorities involved? Are you OK sis? Give me a sign or a silent signal if you are in distress! Who can do that everyday Monday thru Friday and be OK? My favorite response was when I had one mom tell me that she parks her car, gets out and goes and talks to another mom who is in her car. OK, so, let me understand this, you get to school an hour before your kid gets out. You get on the "Porch" and are fifth in line. You put your car in park and get out. You then proceed to walk back to the car that is parked in the tenth spot on the "Porch" and you proceed to get in her car. So, what are you two chatting about for an hour?

Well this is where it gets funny. I was told they talk about the upcoming holiday festivities at school. Again, it's August and the first "Holiday" is Halloween and that is in October, ummm OK. They also talk about who didn't respond in the group text, discuss homework concerns, teacher complaints, playdates, practices and random other shit. I asked my mom friend, "So do you all talk about this stuff because you didn't get a chance to talk about it earlier in the day because of work?" She says, "No, we did talk about it earlier in the day via text, but we wanted to discuss it in person." "Wait, didn't you say all you needed to say to each other about these topics via text message?" "Yes, but it is not the same, and we have no time in the day to talk to one another." "Wait, yes, you do have time in the day to talk, if you were texting all day about the same shit. Why didn't you just call each other?" She says, "I don't know, it is just easier to text sometimes and this way we have something to discuss as we wait for dismissal." "Wait, that makes no sense, if you talked about all of this stuff earlier, then how do you have something to discuss later?"

I give up at that point, walk away and shake my head. I then stopped, turned around and asked, "Did you work today?" She responds, "Oh, no I don't work, remember?" I literally started laughing and said, "OMG, then you had all day to talk to your friend but you decide the best time to do it is to park your car, walk back to her car and gossip for an hour about shit you already discussed, that could have been discussed over lunch, over the phone or later on that day, but you decided to do it in the pick-up line and, to make matters worse, you were so busy gossiping that you didn't get back to your car in time and so you are now holding up all of the other parents, who are trying to make it to their appointment that they ridiculously scheduled for 15 minutes after dismissal and they are already on edge and ready to curse the first person who jeopardizes their on-time arrival. OK, sis, you do what you do and good luck with all that." Moms, we can definitely #SURVIVE the pick-up line, just pack your patience, your humor and your snack. The snack may either be used to provide nutrients for this long haul, or it may be used as part of your "theater" snack as you watch shit unfold in the pick-up line. Either way, you will be OK and it's just another lesson in #SURVIVIN'.

SURVIVIN' THE PTA
AND BEING A ROOM PARENT (RP)

SO, WE ALL ARE FAMILIAR WITH THE PARENT TEACHER Association (PTA) and being a Room Parent (RP). Do you know the difference between them? If not, let me try to explain. I am sure someone will have a problem with my explanation/definition, and I could care less.

So, the PTA is a group of parents who volunteer their time to participate in school events that can include but are not limited to dances, bake sales, holiday celebrations for the entire school or grade, and so on. The PTA has several positions that are chosen by voting amongst their PTA peers. There is usually a President, Vice President, Treasurer, and then there are Chairs and Co-Chairs for various activities that happen throughout the school year. At my school, the most important Chair position was the Fifth Grade Chair, because that meant you automatically get access to the end-of-the-year field trip and social event/dance/party. My mom friends have shared some rough stories about the savageness of their schools' PTA president and Chairs of various activities. I literally laugh because I always say, this shit will never happen to me because the universe knows better. I will drive behind the bus on the way to the theme park, so don't worry, I will be there without your permission or approval.

Room Parent (RP) is a position that is chosen by the classroom teacher, because either A, she really likes you and would love the support and assistance during this crazy school year, or B, you bothered the shit out of her all summer long including the first three days of school, so she chose your ass to get some mental stability before she has to go and teach your child. The RP is the gateway between the teacher and the other parents. They are responsible for many things like distributing important class information regarding field trips, class pictures, holiday activities, and so on. The RP may have the ability to choose three or four other parents to serve as room assistants. The room assistants help with art projects, class pictures, field trips and other activities that the RP either doesn't want to do or has no time to do. If you don't get chosen to be a RP and you really feel the need to be involved, you may get lucky and be chosen as a room assistant, so let's hope that you and the RP get along and don't have bad blood.

Being a part of the PTA or being an RP are both considered volunteer positions within our children's school. They are my least favorite part of the parental school experience. It's not because I don't like activities, fun, other parents (well maybe a few) or the school. It's just that once you get involved, it doesn't seem like volunteer work anymore and most people forget that possibly one out of the twenty parents who are on the PTA or the one parent who is chosen as the RP, may have a damn job, full time or part time, it doesn't matter. I cannot be here all day is my point. That one parent is me. I have the damn job. I work eight a.m. until four p.m. every day, and after that I have the pleasure of driving an Uber pool for about three to four hours without compensation for three or four small people. I am the parent that runs, yes RUNS, to her car after BTSN (Back to School Night). I am the parent who avoids eye contact on the "Porch" with the lady wearing her Lulu Lemon workout clothes and holding a bright green pamphlet to hand out to each and every parent/guardian at drop off, that explains all of the reasons to be involved in the PTA.

I am the parent that avoids making friends with the moms who are hoping to be chosen as RP because I don't want you to think you can pick me to be a room assistant. I am that parent. My mom friends are that parent. You know why we are those parents? Because if we have a job or not, we are not in the business of making this volunteer but not volunteer commitment part of our daily routine. I get enough spam emails; I don't have time for more. WE also feel that once we drop those kids off at school, we don't have to see them again for six hours, and for us, that is a great feeling. Some of you guys act like you don't need a break from your kid. I am not included in that group. I get mad when I see the school calendar and count all of the Teacher Planning Days (TPDs) and realize they added two extra ones this year, so I have two less days of being in my own space, doing what I want to do in my own time, without my damn kids complaining, crying, screaming, fighting or doing whatever to get my blood pressure high. So, no I do not want to join the PTA or be an RP because ya'll don't know how to act.

When I say they make the volunteer job less volunteering and more mandatory, let me explain myself. What has happened to me in the past, and a few of my mom friends who are trying to #SURVIVE the school year, is that once we get in, we can't get out. It's like a cult. They have their leader, and they do whatever he/she says, and they have no say in how shit pans out. That doesn't work for me. For one, I am a whole adult, so no other adult is going to demand that I stand outside of the school and pass out flyers for shit from eight to nine a.m. and from three to four p.m. For two, I am a whole adult, like I said before, and no one will be calling me all hours of the day, asking me if I read the email, or if I have prepared the art supplies for the activity that the class is doing in three weeks. For three, I am a whole adult and not one person will tell me what I can and cannot pack in my child's lunch box. My kid doesn't have an allergy, so why can't she eat her favorite sandwich at lunch time, because the kid in the cafeteria who sits six tables back is allergic to wheat, soy, eggs, cheese, meat, nuts, water and shit anything else? I have a hard enough time trying to pack a lunch that my kid will not waste, and now you are telling me that I have to stop sending the one thing my kid actually eats because of a kid who is not even in my kid's grade, let alone, in their class? This is too much people. Like seriously, my job is easier than this shit.

Now let me share something that has caused a few of my mom friends to have more enemies at school than friends. Well remember when I said that you are usually chosen by the teacher to be a RP? Well for some ODD reason, these mamas show EVERY OUNCE OF INTEREST in being the RP that the teacher ends up always emailing them to ask if they would like to be the RP instead of really "choosing" one because she is worn down and tired of the spam emails. Well played mamas, well played! I used to wonder why she chose them. Not because they are not worthy, but because they literally stalked the teacher day and night. Why did she choose the one who was literally at her doorstep every morning and afternoon, fighting for her love, attention and slight favor? My one good girlfriend is so crazy about being the RP that she starts scanning the room and looking at all of the parents' social media, that are in her kid's class. IG and Facebook will tell you a lot about a person if you really need to know. You all need to do better about putting all of your business in the streets. Anyway, I digress, so after a few minutes of trolling, she realizes that the competition is stiff, and she is not the only one who wants the job. There are so many other parents who have nothing else to do all day, so this is pure fun and joy for them. I am not about that life, people, so leave me alone! I am NOT interested! They are wide open from drop-off to pick-up. They need to fill their time during the day in between shopping and working out so they have to be at school telling everyone else what to do. They want to see their kids the entire time they are at school. I am like six hours without my kids is a vacation, why would I want to voluntarily give that up when it's mandatory for them to go to school without me? Yeah, no, I'll pass. Hence, I never got asked!

For an RP, the teacher usually wants someone low key and low maintenance. They want someone who will let them teach and will speak when spoken to or requested, per se. They do not want someone who feels that they need to change the culture of the classroom, have a say so about tests/quizzes and homework. They really want someone who would just send an email here or there, tell parents to sign up for shit when needed and just allow them to teach. My girlfriend realized, she can do all of those things on her teacher's bucket list and that's why she was asked me to be the RP. Now the real problem came when the other parents realized that she was chosen as RP and they are pissed at her and talking about her to everyone else. They are outraged. They feel blindsided. She hears the chatter amongst the other parents. They stop talking when she walks by. They look away from her when she catches them staring at her on the "Porch" as she pushes her kids out of the car. When they finally accept that she is the RP, they start to be her best friend. They start taking an interest in her job and her kids. Lady, you have never spoken to her before, and her kids have been in the same class with your kids since Kinder. Do you even know her name? No, because you two are not cool. They have nothing to talk about. But they keep talking to her because they want her to choose them as a room assistant. They know she has three spots to fill and this decision is all hers.

So, after careful thought and consideration, she accepts the position as RP for the fourth-grade class. She also takes the liberty and enjoyment of filling the three spots for room assistants. So, I'm sure you are wondering who she will make the room assistants. In her heart she secretly wished her mom friends were in class with her so that she could be selfish and choose them. But unfortunately, they are not. So, at this point she has to take a few moments and analyze her options. She needs someone who is good at art, someone who loves to organize baskets and shit and someone who is so desperate to be in the class that they don't care what she assigns them to assist with, they will do it. Now we all know that the person who is the most desperate is the one who has been stalking the teacher since they found out their kid was in their class. I mean, they are being nice and shit to her and did offer to provide anything she needs for the class supply list, if they don't get enough donations. They make sure that just in case she needs any support, because they have done this before, they provide her with their Snapchat—lady, she doesn't snap anyone—they have already requested her on Facebook and are following her on Instagram.

Uuumm...yeah, she is thinking to herself, I don't like you like that, and I certainly don't know you, so why would we be Fakebook, I mean Facebook friends and follow each other on IG? But nonetheless, she gave her the spot. Now the next person she chooses has to really love art or just pretend they do. Why? Because she can't draw, she does NOT do projects unless they are for a grade (yes that statement means she, just like the rest of us, do projects, because we all know we do those kids' projects for them, we don't have time for bullshit, so we just get it done with our non-dominant hand). She needs this specific type of room assistant because for some reason, for each holiday there is some type of class project that needs to be done so the Principal can put it up in the hallway for all to see. Most of the shit just comes home and we put it up for a few months and then it goes to that project storage bin in the basement, attic or office. If I get one more holiday ring for the tree, or another Thanksgiving laminated place mat with my baby's handprint on it, I may just lose my mind. I mean, I love the thought and all, but with three kids who all have or had to go through Kinder, first, second, third, fourth, and fifth grade, I think I have enough placemats for a dining hall that seats 300 people. I'm just saying. So, anyways, this person has no problem coming up with ideas and gathering the supplies for it. They love to do it, because once they gather it all up, they get to deliver it to the classroom and sneak a peek at their kid. Now the last spot she needs to fill is for that one parent who loves to put baskets and shit together. They love themes and school functions. The person she chooses for this will be dedicated to their school carnival theme and the assigned basket they have to present for their class. They are really good about getting donations of gift cards, wine and goods.

So now that I have analyzed her room parent assistants, let me tell you what she does next. She lets her teacher know who she chose so she can send that passive-aggressive email to all of them, including herself, but we know she is not directing her passive-aggressiveness towards her because they got an understanding. The email basically says, Hello, welcomes them to her class, thanks them for their time in volunteering this year. She lets them know that she has already chosen a room parent, my friend, and the room parent, again that's my friend, has chosen her three room assistants. She lets them know why she needs a room parent and it's because they assist her with day-to-day operations that are outside of teaching their children the fundamental concepts that lie within the core subject areas needed for academic growth and achievement. She also lets them all know that if there are any questions or concerns, please direct them to her room parent, my friend, and the room parent, remember that is my friend, will consult with her and she will let the entire class know the decision or outcome.

The most important thing she says is that the room assistants are just that, assistants, and she hopes that they will be an asset to her room parent— ahhh, that is my FRIEND. She ends with letting them know that a meeting will be scheduled soon to discuss the upcoming event. What she is saying is don't email her to ask her about Halloween, we are in August and right now I need to get through this first math lesson because we have a test coming up next week. She sees them all at pick up and they are smiling at her and they appear to be happy. Shit, she doesn't care if they are, she is so fucking happy she is in charge! She is not happy because they smiled or spoke to her for once. She is happy because when she is at work doing her shit, they are at school doing her other shit for her. It's a win-win for her and maybe a win for them, it all depends on how they look at it. Glass half full or half empty. I would go with half full so they can get through the school year, because she is the HRPIC (Head Room Parent In Charge), SUCKAS.

Now the day comes that they have a meeting with the teacher, and she makes it quite clear that all things go thru the RP. She will filter things through my friend to be distributed to the rest of the class. She also makes sure to let them know that she cannot be disturbed throughout the day because she has the important task of teaching our kids. So, she is basically saying, "Leave me alone!" They respect it but you will always have that one parent who wants to be in charge even though they are not. They send emails requesting shit from parents without her knowledge. They collect money and don't turn it in to her for the class funds. Oh, and they are the ones who are ballsy enough to ask the teacher to change a test because they are going on a vacation for the long weekend. Umm, even if you were the RP, that is unacceptable and for you to have the audacity to ask that is absurd. Seriously, this shit happens just like this every year!

This is when shit gets real because she has to set some people straight and remind them who the HRPIC is, yet again. She holds a meeting and the first thing she says is, "Please run me my money!" Well, she says it in a calmer, more sophisticated way, so she says, "I understand money was collected for the end of the year celebration, can you please Venmo today?" She reminds them that the teacher only wants her to send emails to the parents because she doesn't want confusion. All emails are filtered through her so that she is aware of what is going on just in case it gets to administration. Lastly, she makes sure to remind them that they cannot under any circumstances ask for favors to accommodate their kids when it comes to homework or testing because they don't want their kids to be behind the other fourth-grade classes when it comes to state testing. She also makes sure to mention that it also violates the bylaws the PTA has set for room parents and room assistants, and she is sure that they all want to be there and part of the daily class routine. They give her the side-eye, she doesn't care, and she politely tells them, thank you and she will see them at pick-up because she has to get back to work. This, my friends, is why I don't have too many parent friends at school. Well, actually I do have many parent friends, but they are just like me #SURVIVIN' being a room parent. We text one another after our respective meetings, we send one another secret pictures taken at drop-off and pick-up, we call each other and gossip about the shit that happened today, all while we continue to lift one another up and help each other get through the day. When I can call my girlfriends and talk shit and laugh about the stupid chaos a mom caused at school, it makes this whole thing called parenting a whole lot easier. Don't forget to use that one lifeline we all have: Phone a Friend. It is the key to #SURVIVIN' these days.

SURVIVIN' HOMEWORK AND PROJECTS

I HATE HOMEWORK AND FUCKING SCHOOL PROJECTS. I have no idea how I #SURVIVED and how my kids #SURVIVED. It is always a struggle, but I can say, the older they get the less of a struggle it is. I know this because I don't have as many freak-outs and panic attacks as I use to. My girlfriends with kids younger than mine, are struggling, I mean struggling. My girlfriends with kids older than mine are maintaining and thriving. I am almost maintaining but I am still struggling. Trust me when I say, you will be OK. It does get better, I promise. Just believe and you will achieve. That sounded like an infomercial. But it's a motto to live by when you are raising kids.

So, let's start talking about this homework. Do you all remember the poem, or shall I say, have you heard of the poem, "Homework Oh Homework" by Jack Prelutsky? It goes like this:

"Homework! Oh, Homework. I hate you! You stink! I wish I could wash you away in the sink. If only a bomb would explode you to bits. Homework! Oh, Homework! You're giving me fits. I'd rather take baths with a man-eating shark or wrestle a lion alone in the dark, eat spinach and liver, pet ten porcupines, then tackle the homework my teacher assigns. Homework! Oh, Homework! You're last on my list; I simply can't see why you even exist. If you just disappeared, it would tickle me pink. Homework! Oh, Homework! I hate you! You stink!"

I don't know or care about how the kids feel, but this is my feeling exactly on this new-age homework our kids are getting sent home. So, amongst my group of girlfriends we have separate issues with homework, but we all agree we HATE IT! IT STINKS! For one of my girlfriends, her kids go to a great school. The teachers are teaching; hence the kids are learning. But with all that teaching and learning, comes homework. The amount of homework her children get is out of hand. It's like you hate it and love it at the same damn time. Yes, you want your kids to flourish and make gains in their educational growth, but why does it seem like the only way it can happen is if the kid gets eight pages of math problems, three chapters to read in Science, two short stories to read for Language Arts, along with comprehension questions, plus two projects due Monday and don't forget they have to do an hour of math on this fucked-up computer program and read a book they picked out from the library that is not within their reading range, and take a quiz. I mean, don't get me wrong, I think homework is valuable to learning, but this shit is excessive. Why are you assigning homework for Spring Break?

I mean it would be acceptable if it was just maybe one or two worksheets, but no, these people send home 100-page review packets because when we return from break, it's state testing time and we are losing a week of school. My question to the teachers is, so in one week, which is five days, if there was no break, how were you going to get through all of these concepts in this packet? How? I need to know, because if my kid can comprehend all that shit in five days, why can't they comprehend anything that I have been telling them on repeat for the last eight years of their life? Are you going to be doing homework during your Spring Break? Are your kids, who also go to this school, going to be doing this 100-page packet while on Spring Break? Let me answer those last two for you. HELL NO! I know this because you and I have been friends on Facebook and IG for over three years now, before my kid had you as a teacher. So, as I sit in the pick-up line one hour before dismissal, I have nothing else to do but scroll social media, remember. So, you have already posted on Facebook how excited you are for your seven-day Western Caribbean cruise. You are packed and ready to go! You even have a countdown and currently it is sitting at twenty-six hours. So, sis, explain to me why my kid has to do it and your kid doesn't and it is for a damn grade.

OK, give them an F if you want to. That is all I am going to say about that shit! Just in case you were wondering we left for our vacation #unbothered and stress free! Now on the other hand, my twins went to a school with a No-homework policy. OK, yes, I know this sounds great to most parents, but let me let you in on a little secret, that shit is a setup. How can kids not have any homework in Math? I mean its math they need something to keep up with the concepts, right? I am no teacher, but I have no idea how you are supposed to really learn something with no homework at all. What really got me is that this was not something that was only for the elementary grades, this shit was through eighth grade. Ummm…this is middle school, they can get homework now, please. I know it sounds like I am contradicting myself, because I said earlier, I hate homework. I do, that will never change. Let me explain why I hate it so much. But this isn't rocket science, people, you need homework for repetition and comprehension. It doesn't have to be pages and pages, but damn, something is always better than nothing, right?

I hate homework because I cannot understand how teachers send homework home with no lesson plans or parent Cliff Notes. How am I supposed to help this kid if I have no Idea of how you presented it or taught it in class? I mean, can't we livestream with the option of recording the lessons, so the parents have a damn reference point? I am asking for a friend. That friend is me! I am that friend. I have literally had to walk away from the table with my kids because they are mad at me because I don't understand how to do the math problems. I am like OK, this looks like it is above my pay grade, but let's see what I can do. So, I do what I always do as an adult who has to tackle children's problems, I use Google. I will Google the hell out of a math concept, science lesson, vocabulary word, spelling words. Shit, I have no shame. I learned this shit at least thirty years ago and it was not taught like this. I have no idea what that word is, let alone tell you whether it is a verb, adjective, preposition, pronoun or whatever else they need to know. I only know words that I can spell and sound out. So, I started my Google search for this advanced math concept and then I started watching videos and shit.

I am like, "Oh, OK, I remember this, this is easier than I thought." I realized that I knew an easier way to do this, so I said to my kid, "OK, mommy knows how to do this. Let me show you!" I'm excited, right, I am thinking to myself, you are going to kill this lesson and you are going to show your kid that they can come to you for any math help they may need. You get your paper and pencil and start to write the problem down and then you start with the first step and all of a sudden, out of nowhere, they start yelling at you saying "Mommy, that is not how the teacher showed us in class! Stop! You are doing it wrong!"

Wait, hold up, what the hell just happened? I politely take a pregnant pause, gather all of my thoughts together and inhale, exhale, inhale, exhale. One more time for good measure, I inhale and then slowly exhale. I am doing all this just with the hope that my child realizes that they may need to either back up, retract the last statement, or run. But they don't, so I do the long mom stare-down and I say, "Hold up, wait a minute! How the hell are you going to tell me that I am not doing it like the teacher did it, when your little ass obviously didn't remember how the teacher did it, because you came to me for assistance? If she was so good at teaching you, then you wouldn't be stressing me while I am trying to cook dinner for you. If you really under-stood the concept that she was teaching you, you would have learned it in class and again, not interrupting me and asking me for help. If my way is not the way the teacher showed you in class, then why did you bother me, AGAIN, while I was trying to cook dinner for you?" My kid doesn't even flinch. They huff and puff, which makes me so mad that I literally start look-ing around the room, making sure that there is no one else that this huffing and puffing could be directed at, but nope, it's just me. I tell my child, OK, well let's take a beat and look at the example and the problem again and let me try to explain it better. I start my first step over again, and this little shit starts yelling at me to stop, like I am about to walk out in front of a moving train or something. I say, "OMG, stop the damn screaming, please! What is the problem? You asked me for help, I try to help you and then you tell me my help is wrong!" Why am I here? Why did you call me over here? Why am I not in the kitchen finishing up my new recipe?

So, we are going back and forth and finally I lose my shit and I say, "Fuck it! You do it yourself since I can't seem to do it like your teacher, who sent your little ass home with no notes, no lesson plans, nada. OK, and make sure you tell her tomorrow when you have to turn in your assignment that it's all wrong because your mom said since she can't clone you, she told you to wait until you see her again to get help with this new concept." Yep I said that shit to my kid and I don't regret it.

But wait for it. The shit hits the fan and causes an unexpected explosion when my husband walks downstairs, and he ask me why I am screaming and why am I not trying to listen to our child so I can help them understand the math concept better. Yep, he did that shit, moms. I said, "Oh, my bad, do you know how to do this math concept taught today?"

He says "No, I don't know what it is about."

I said, "Here take a look and maybe you can help them understand it better."

He comes over to the table and looks at the example, same shit I did, then he looks at the problem, same shit I did, then he pulls out his phone and starts to Google the concept, you know, same shit I did, and then he says, "Oh I know how to do this. This is easy, baby, let me show you how to do it!" He starts on the first step, same shit I did, and as he is starting to explain it as he is writing it down, same shit I did, they say in the rudest voice ever, "Daddy, that is not correct, you are doing it wrong!" You thought I lost my shit, hahaha, I just sat back and watched it unfold. He says, "Wait a damn minute here, if you can tell me I am doing it wrong, then you don't need my help, right? If you are not happy with my answer, then why did you ask for my help?"

My kid says, "Daddy, I didn't ask you for help, you interrupted mommy trying to help me and you offered!"

DEAD! I had to walk away from the table because I was dying of laughter, like tears were falling from my eyes, because I was so happy that this shit happened to another adult in this house besides me. I get so tired of telling my husband about this homework shit and then he looks at me and says, "You need to have more patience with the kids. You let them get to you and you are the adult. You need to stop letting them tell you what they want you to do and just do it; you are an adult." You know I wanted to repeat that same shit to his ass that day, but I didn't because I was not mentally prepared for a grown man tantrum at this point. I was not about to tackle four kids today, when I was only mentally prepared to tackle three. So, I just looked at him because I wanted to see the reaction to that response. He said, "Fine, if you don't like how I am helping you, then don't ask me for help anymore. Mommy is trying to help you and you are telling her it isn't good enough. Daddy tried to help, and you said the same thing. So, from now on, make sure you understand that shit before you get home."

He was pissed, rightfully so, but I was still laughing my ass off, because it was a priceless moment and I am sure it will be another twenty light years before it happens again. Have you ever heard that saying, "Stay out of grown folk's business?" If so, this is the lesson he learned that day. Stay out of mom life business. This shit ain't for the faint at heart or for everyone. You have no idea how to #SURVIVE the homework woes, so please don't try again. If I ask you for your assistance, then you can step in; if not, please give me FIDDY feet and DO NOT PASS GO, DO NOT COLLECT TWO HUNDRED DOLLARS. YOU GONNA LEARN TODAY MR! YOU GONNA LEARN TODAY!

Who thought that school projects were a great idea to add to the essence of learning? I will find you and I will hurt you! I don't recall doing school projects back in my day and I am just fine. This new age school project shit is my nemesis. I know that every teacher out there knows that when you assign a project, that shit is intended for the parents. I will not go into serious detailed explanations about specific situations that have come up in my life, my mom friends' lives or anyone who actually cares about a mom's mental state. But what I will do is ask a few questions, with a few short follow-up responses, because I am 100% sure I am not the only one who is thinking this shit. I am asking for a student. That student is me. I am that student doing this project at forty years old for the third fucking time as a parental unit.

Science fair projects can kick rocks with open-toed shoes, right? Why do I have to do a NEW science fair project for second through tenth grades? Why can't the science project that I did for my now-eighth grader, not be used for my now third grader? Why are these new age-technology teachers asking for PowerPoints instead of poster boards? Why are you making me do Science Fair projects about things that I really don't care about? Why do you think that I can come up with a hypothesis on my own? I can't, so please supply more than five choices when you have more than five kids in your class. Why am I doing a science fair project for my tenth grader? Just so we are clear, I will be doing the same project I did in third grade because you have no idea.

These ridiculous monthly themed projects are a joke, right? Why are we making tombstones in sixth grade for Halloween? I don't want to make a tombstone about a dead person. Isn't that like bad juju or something like that? Why are we making two-dimensional dolls to represent Hispanic heritage month? What is the point of that project? What pisses me off the most is that these damn teachers like to give restrictions and some even go as far as to tell you the exact type of material and shit you have to use. Umm. Wait a minute, the Dollar Store has many items for a dollar. Why do I need to spend twenty dollars at Michael's when I can get the same shit at the Dollar Store? Why are you telling me what brand of markers to use? It's a marker, they all do the same shit.

If you didn't do a lesson on Poems, why are you assigning a random poem for an assignment? Why are you asking me to draw a picture to describe my poem? I can't draw! My kid can't even draw a stick figure, so what the Hell! My kid has no idea how to write a poem, so it's OK to make the assumption that you know the parents are going to write this shit for them, right? They think Dr. Seuss books are poems, so all they will do is start rhyming simple words like cat, hat, ball, fall, toe, foe and so on. Why are you assigning projects that include wetlands, drylands, caves, hills, valleys, shit anything that involves the earth? Isn't one science project enough? The fair should count as ten science projects spread out over two years. Again, my kid cannot draw, and neither can I, so who do you think is going to draw this grassy wetland with animals and shit?

Quick poll here, who can write a bibliography without using Google right now? I'll wait.. Exactly, none of you suckers, so why is this even a request? Umm, this is third grade, lady. I didn't learn how to write a proper bibliography until my second year of college, and I am just fine, and I used the internet to assist me and the cheat sheet my college professor gave me and the entire English class. So, tell me again, why is this needed at such a young, tender age of eight? Tell me again, why you tell me I can use the internet to find sources and then you say, but you can't use Wikipedia? Who does that? That is pure evil and not very Christian-like. If I use Wikipedia to see if Kim Kardashian's butt is real, then why don't you think I am going to use it for this specific situation? Everyone uses Wikipedia; it's a valuable resource these days. Who still has *Encyclopedia Britannica*? Why do my kids need to know how to compose a musical composition when they don't even know how to play an instrument? They listen to Spotify night and day and probably during your class, because there are these things called "AirPods" that are all the craze these days!

Projects are a set-up. They are done to piss the parents off. What really frustrates me is when that one mom likes to start a group chat to complain about the project and how she has no time, it is so ridiculous, and she is boycotting the shit and turning in whatever. Then her overachieving, ass-kissing, teacher's pet, trying to secure that room-mom spot next year for her other child, current room assistant ass, ends up bringing a damn project that outshines everybody and I swear on everything I love, she paid a professional artist to create the design and also a professional journalist to write the synopsis and all the other written work. It's fucking amazing, I cannot deny that, but it is fucking UNNECESSARY! So, then the shady-ass project-giving teacher gives great praise to that kid in class in front of all of the other kids whose parents worked equally hard on their kids' projects. Saying that this is the perfect example of following the directions and using all of the required items on the list, blah blah blah... Our kids are not happy with the extra star in the journal, but they all decided, via a visual survey, to not say anything or make a scene in class, at the lunch table or at recess. Just let it go and all will be good. We are very happy with our regular "A" with no star in the journal. Shit, my kid would be happy with a "B," but he knows that when mommy does projects she expects nothing less than an "A." But we all have that one kid who can't just go with the flow and decides to open their big-ass trouble-starting, instigating mouth and say, "We all know you didn't do that project. We all know your mom did it because your mom called our moms and asked them if they were using markers or crayons and if they knew exactly where to find the resources to write about the wetland." That one kid with the big-mouth, the trouble-starting and instigating-mouth-ass kid, is my kid. My kid is the one who can't just let it go. So then all of the other kids decide to blow the whistle and tell the teacher that they also know that he didn't do his project because last night when they were playing Fortnite on Xbox Live, while ALL of their moms were doing the project due today, he was telling all of them that his mom had some fancy people over with art supplies and stuff and kept asking him to come downstairs to write certain things with a pencil.

OOOOOOOOOOWEEEEEEEEEEE, a soup sandwich has been delivered. The teacher is pissed at this point because she feels that no one took the project seriously and telling them that their parents cannot keep doing their homework forever, blah blah blah... So, she gives everyone an "F." Hold up, lady, you knew when you assigned this ridiculous shit that these kids were not even going to attempt to do it. You knew that when you assigned it along with those long-ass instructions, these kids would be lost. You knew that when you said it was due next week, Monday, and you assigned it this week on Friday, those kids were not going to do it. So, if you knew all that, why are you mad? My hard work, dedication, time, frustrations, fingertips, manicure, pedicure, massage and facial all had something to do with this assignment getting done and turned in on time. I deserve an "A," damnit. I deserve an "A" for effort, an "A" for my time and an "A" for a bomb-ass project. So, give me, I mean my child, an A and govern yourself accordingly. Thank you and Goodnight!

Oh, and by the way, we took a group vote, and we deleted her ass from the group chat and ignored her in the drop-off line, pick-up line and the PTA meetings. We are out here living our best lives trying to #SURVIVE, so if you think that is your way of #SURVIVIN', you do you honey, and these school streets are going to eat you alive really quick. So, moms, yes, we may hate school projects, but we just have to bang them out. The thing to remember is NEVER THROW THAT SHIT OUT! NEVER DELETE THAT POWER-POINT! NEVER GIVE UP. #SURVIVIN' is what we do and what we are good at. That's exactly why we are thriving now!

SURVIVIN' PUBERTY

SO, I HAVE BEEN THROUGH THE TEEN STAGE COMPLETELY once with one child and I am going through it again with my last two. Mom, I apologize for my behavior as an adolescent teen who was going through this stage. It's no fun when you are on this side, the parent side. I have two girls and one boy. Oh, how I love my kids, but boys are much easier in my opinion than girls when it comes to this place in the game. Thankfully, I have my husband who can deal with the boy stuff as I deal with the girl stuff. So, it is all fun and games until your pediatrician says, "Oh, I see buds! She will get her menstrual cycle soon."

Wait, back that up, what did you just say? My baby is only ten and I didn't get my period until I was thirteen, almost fourteen, so what are you talkin' about, Willis? I not only heard this once, but twice and I was not happy or accepting of it either time. Who wants to start having the period talk with their fifth grader? Not me! Who wants to show your ten-year-old how to put on a pad correctly and how to know when to change it? Not me! So, since no one is volunteering for this role, why are we discussing this, Doc? So thankfully both of my girls spared me, and it didn't happen until twelve. I would have loved thirteen, but it is what it is. It was still a hard conversation to have at twelve, but I'm sure it was way better than if I would have had to do it at ten. I got a two-year preparation period.

So, before the period comes, like maybe three to six months before, you are already mentally preparing yourself because you see the mood swings and aggressive behavior. You get attitude for just asking what they want for dinner. They start taking slightly longer in the bathroom in the morning, and stuff like that. All of sudden, shopping at Justice isn't allowed anymore and they want their entire room repainted and rebranded. But you love pink and purple and all of your cute pillows and stuffed animals (insert death stare by tween-age daughter)! So, the day you have been dreading has finally come. For me, both of my girls had this unwanted parental moment happen while they were at my cousin's house. It was not that bad for my oldest, because I was there with her and I had my supply bag with me, as I don't leave home without it. We went in the bathroom and had a short discussion. I had extra clothes with me anyway, because it was a pool party, so all was falling into place.

My second one was so extra. She was at my cousin's house, but I was not there. She was staying over. So, I was minding my own business, watching my housewives and other reality television shows and I started getting all of these spam text messages. Like they were coming back to back. The only thing the first thirty said was, "MOMMYYYYYYYYYYYYYYYYYYYYYYYYY YYYYYYYYYYYYYYYYYYYYYYYYYYYYYYYYYYYYYY! Seriously, I got thirty texts just like that, and then I got "I'M BLEEDINGGGGGGGGGGG-GGGG! about twenty times. I was like OK, give me a minute to gather myself. I immediately texted my cousin and said, "We have a code red in one of your bathrooms!" She texted back and said, "OK, I'm on the hunt, with supplies in hand!" That's how we roll. We are always there for each other when needed, no questions asked. After that, I attempted to call my child and she kept side-buttoning me. Which means she didn't want to talk to me on the phone, she only wanted to text me. I was thinking I cannot help you via text, we need some verbal discussions, maybe even FaceTime. So, I Facetimed her and she declined me again. So, I had to text her ass and say, "Answer the phone so I can help you." She texted back, "I'm busy." I'm thinking, what are you doing that has you so busy, because from what I know we haven't gotten anywhere in our discussions and you should have zero clue about what to do. Well it turned out, she had Googled it and called her older sister for assistance and had the nerve to tell her that I was not responding to her text messages and she couldn't call my cousin because she didn't have her number so she called her sister. So thankfully, my oldest, who is six years older, was able to calm her down and get her to unlock the bathroom door so she could get the supplies she needed and a clean change of clothes as well as call her mama back to inform her of the update.

After about thirty minutes I was able to make contact. I had permission and a window of opportunity. She scolded me for not answering her fifty spam text messages fast enough. She scolded me for not having her prepared and she scolded me for trying to take her home. So, my cousin lives about an hour away from me, so when we get our kids together, it's like Christmas for them. They act like we deprive them of family interaction just to punish them. So when I asked her politely and in a concerned parent voice, "Baby, do you want mommy to come and pick you up so you can be home right now?" she started screaming and said, "Why would you come get me right now? If you come get me, I can't stay the night? Are you going to bring me back up here after I come home? Why did you ask me that?"

I was shook at that point, because it was like I was talking to the devil on speaker phone. Her tone was not OK, her voice was loud, and I could feel her glaring at me through the phone. I was like, "OK, well I will be there early tomorrow to get you all, ok?"

She said, "Don't come too early, we need time to play, and since you didn't prepare me for this, I lost about four hours of playing time with my favorite cousin."

Again, I was shook. So, I was just like, "OK, I will get there when I get there," and hung up before she could offer any rebuttal. But please note, her little sassy ass made sure to text me not to come early, call before I come, and don't drive fast, take my time. I knew at that moment; this puberty shit is going to be a fucking nightmare with this one.

Since the periods have arrived, we have had many ups and downs with attitudes, behaviors and moments. I have mastered both girls' mood swings the week before the red sea arrives to shore. I prepare the men in the house because they have no idea what is about to happen for the next seven to ten days in this house. It just so happens that after about a year, both girls are a week apart, so it really is about fourteen days of hell in our house. The emotions go from high to low in zero to sixty seconds, with no warning. If I ask them if they need supplies, they bite my head off, so I no longer ask them. I just stockpile those bitches under my sink. My younger one shares a bathroom with her twin brother, so I had to politely tell her that when it's that time, maybe use your sister's bathroom so we don't traumatize him. They both hated that idea and said, why do we have to change for him? He needs to change for us. I was like OK, I don't have time for this girl power shit right now. I have too much shit going on. The number of times I have been given the death stare for asking them to hurry up and come downstairs to eat my gourmet breakfast before we leave for school, is borderline parental abuse. My son just looks at them and shakes his head. He always makes comments, like you two are so mean to mom and you need to be nicer to her. They annihilate his ass right there at the kitchen table, two against one. They even go off on each other most days because they both need to feel validated and right. It's ridiculous. I only had a brother, so shit was pretty cut and dry in my house. Let's just say this about this topic, been there done that and still doing it but I'm #SURVIVIN'. That shit is and still is rough, but I'll be alright.

OK, we all know that as women, we love clothes, fashion, trends, make-up and all that fancy and fun shit. Some of us are a little more into it than others, and that is OK. But when you are going through the teen stage, it gets exhausting. Thankfully, my two are not DIVAS but they do love certain pampering options like hair and nails but nothing that makes me have to re-evaluate my finances to keep up with their beauty regimens. They both love clothes and shoes. It is so funny watching them wear things that were in style back in our days. They swear it is new and that they are wearing it better than we ever did. What makes me laugh is when I buy myself some high-waisted jeans or a cute pair of high-fashion sneakers and they comment with, "Ooohhhh look at mom, being all trendy!" I look at them like, little girl this ain't nothing new, I have always had good style. Shit you have never looked a mess, hence why you have such great style these days. We have had some arguments about clothing but nothing too bad. My girls also know that I do not have any problem saying NO and I will do it in multiple settings, in multiple voices and accompanied with multiple facial expressions. So, they don't try me as much as they used to. They are over my rants, rages and out-of-order curse words when I get really mad.

I do have some mom friends who are at the hair and/or nail salon with their tween bi-weekly for a new hairstyle, cut, color or whatever is "On Trend" at the moment. They are constantly battling with their daughter about what they can and can't wear. Just because she is the same age as you and her mom let her "do it for the gram," that isn't how it works over here ma'am. They have told me that they spend fifty to a hundred dollars on new looks for hair or nails at these bi-weekly appointments. Some of them have told me that they have reminders to remember to make their daughter's nail appointment because if they forget, the shit show begins. Excuse me, what shit show? That little girl better take several seats. I asked these specific mom friends if they even like the styles their daughters have chosen. Most say, they would never wear it, or it isn't their cup of tea and some have said that they are jealous that they didn't get it first because it really is cute.

I had one mom who told me to never think about giving your opinion of a look or a style. I was like shit, why not? If I am paying for it, you best believe I'm saying whatever, whenever and wherever I want about how my money is getting spent. She went on to say that one time she gave her daughter her unsolicited opinion on a new haircut and color her daughter thought she wanted, and baaaaabbbbbbyyyyyyy her daughter clapped back at her like she was a stranger off the street. She said she gave her the look of death and said, "OMG mom, who asked you? Please go sit over there and leave me alone. I am not a baby. I don't need your help anymore. Uuuggg Thank you but no thanks."

I was speechless, and if you know me, you know I am very rarely speechless. I have lots to say all the time. I blinked my eyes several times because I thought that it was a dream. I stopped blinking and I said, "Sis, so please tell me you put her ass right back in her place."

She said, "No, I just said, OK, when you don't like it, don't complain to me because I don't want to hear it!"

I stared at her for a good thirty seconds with a look of confusion. I looked around the room because I was trying to get some sort of confirmation that this conversation was between two grown, hard-working, bill-paying, adult females and no children were present at this time. Because from the sound of this conversation we were having, it appeared to me that I was the only grown, hard-working, bill-paying adult in the room and I was having a conversation with a shy, timid, small child between the ages of ten and thirteen. I looked at this woman and started laughing out loud, and I asked her to stop playing with me and tell me what she said in response to her child's attitude about spending her hard-working money.

I felt it was my place and it was the right time to remind her that it was a safe place. I wanted her to know that I was not going to report her or tell anyone outside of the room about how badly she embarrassed her child in public. I wanted her to not feel alone or a bad mom if she felt any shame or regret after she clapped back at her own child as if she was a grown woman. You know, sometimes when you have to put your kids back in a child's place, they have to be reminded that they are the child and you are a whole adult and you will fight them. I have told my kids in public, "I do not get embarrassed in public. You do, OK?" So, after all of my positive affirmations and motivational words of encouragement to make sure she knows I have her back, she proceeds to say, "Girl, you are too funny. No, I told her to not expect me to pay for a new hairstyle or for someone to fix it if she didn't like it. She was annoyed at me for that and so she rolled her eyes and walked away."

At that moment, I realized that she has no idea how to #SURVIVE moments like this. Her idea of #SURVIVIN' this specific type of situation was to not make it a situation. My idea of #SURVIVIN' this kind of situation is by making it a situation. As moms, we can sometimes feel like we don't want to embarrass our kids in public because you may think that it will lead to bullying or something further at the school level. You also may feel that your child is at an age where they can make their own decisions and life choices. Well if you will allow me, let me remind you that YOU ARE A WHOLE ADULT WHO HAS LIVED AND IS STILL LIVING A WHOLE ADULT LIFE. That adult life involves working, cleaning, working, cooking, working, chauffeuring, working, barely eating, working, spending, working, budgeting, working and #SURVIVIN' raising kids.

So, unless your tween/teen is living a WHOLE ADULT LIFE AND IS STILL LIVING A CHILD'S LIFE that involves, working, cleaning, working, cooking, working, chauffeuring, working, barely eating, working, spending, working, budgeting, working and #SURVIVIN' to raise kids, they need to take a beat, pause and re-evaluate their last statement, then RUN…RUN AS FAST AS THEY CAN!! I said, "Girl, if my child felt it in her heart to let that comment slip out of her mouth, remorse or not, I would have let her ass have it and I would give zero fucks. I would remind her that she is my child and just as she talked to you like you were a stranger off the street, I would have talked to her like she was my child who has no job, can't take care of herself in any situation at this point in her life and needs me to survive. My words would go something like this, Let me remind your ass of a few things. First off, you asked me to schedule this appointment after you asked me if you could get your hair done. You also asked me to take you to this appointment because you have no means of transportation. Since this appointment fell on a Saturday, let me remind you that I have plans on Saturdays. Those plans involve me doing absolutely nothing because I do all types of shit Monday thru Friday. Since your appointment is for nine a.m. and your stylist loves to be late for her first appointment, you asked me to go and grab you some Starbucks that you think "we" want. The most important thing that you have asked to do, without saying it out loud, is asking me to pay for this damn hairstyle that you want but will not, I REPEAT, will not be cute on you or anyone who gets it. So little girl, your ass did ask me for my opinion and I just gave it to you. What I am about to give you is a direct command of get your ass up and let's go. You will not disrespect me in public or private, by mouth or by social media. So, until you get your attitude all the way together, you will continue to rock your hair however I tell you to, OK? I said, OK?"

I know, some of you may think that was a little rough. Well I don't, and I will continue to remind my kids that I am the adult and they are the child. Just as my mom did me, and my grandmother did her. Social media and reality television will have our kids thinking that they can say and do whatever they want whenever they want, however they want, with no consequences. They have no idea how much work it takes to provide for them. Unfortunately, girls can make us lose our minds and our religion at the same damn time. But the final reward is so much greater. They may cry, they may be mad at us for a while, but all of these life lessons are good for both of you. They will understand one day how hard you worked and what you did to make things happen. They will understand how you worked so hard to #SURVIVE them and they will thank you for it later. As they get older, they will continue to try your inner gangster, but they will start to learn really quick that your inner gangster is a Real One and plays no games with anyone.

Now for my boy. It was so different. I was told by our pediatrician that he may start doing things little boys do, because they are curious. I politely told him, don't worry, that is NOT my area. Daddy can handle that! There are a few things that I would like to discuss on behalf of the moms out here so we can all be in the know. I am going to do this by asking questions that I have been asked by friends, I have asked myself and that I have asked other human beings. We need answers, and if we can't get answers, we can at least get our questions out there just in case other moms are as confused as we are. I'm sure you all have these same questions but just in case you don't, think of this as "food for thought" per se.

So, first, let's talk about their ability to flagellate on demand and they don't care where they do it at. Why does his entire room smell like an open asshole all day every day? Why does he think that farting in the car with the windows up is funny? Who taught you that? Why is this the "thing" to do? Why do their farts smell like they actually did number two, several times in one sitting? Again, who taught you that? Are you OK? Do we need to see a specialist? Do you not smell that? Did you forget to flush the toilet? No, then why does it smell like a sewer in here? Has your dad smelled your room? No, OK, then maybe he should, and he can explain to me what is happening with your body. No child should have that amount of built-up rotten air to release on demand at this age, right? Did you SHART? Do you even realize how toxic this is to my health? Do you even care? Do you think that girls are attracted to this smell? You know this doesn't work like that Axe commercial, right? Oh, you did, well it doesn't, so stop, OK?

Their inability to smell themselves is mind blowing. Umm, excuse me little boy, but did you put deodorant on today? I am 150% sure that you have travel-size and full-size deodorants at home in at least three places. Those places include your bedroom, bathroom and bookbag. Did you even look in any of those places? No, well I think if you did, then you wouldn't be rotten right now. Let's go back to your room and look again, OK? I know for sure one of those places is on your dresser, where I put it last night next to your uniform. That was my way of reminding you to swipe before you came downstairs. You have only been up for two hours and you smell like you have worked ten long-ass hours in the sun with no breaks. If you smell like this right now, I can only imagine how you will smell after PE or Recess. Baby, do you smell that? No? Well, then I think this deserves a co-payment and a visit, because no twelve-year-old should smell this way first thing in the morning. How many swipes are you using? Are you doing complete swipes, like up and down, or are they little sharp movements? What is that white stuff on the bottom of your shirt, buddy? Deodorant, you say? Well, if that is the case, you somehow missed your entire underarm and only made it to your abdomen. How sway little dude? How sway? I'm totally confused, but I'm trying to understand this, I really am. Help ya mama out here, explain to me what happened? Baby, why do you need another deodorant when I just gave you two brand new ones? You should be good for at least one month, if I am lucky, but two days is not acceptable. How is your deodorant broken? How did you manage to break it into little pieces like this? All you do is take the top off, lift up your arm and swipe in that little crevice a few times, that is all. After that, you put the top back on and go back to whatever you were doing. What did you do different than that? Whatever you did caused this poor deodorant to shred to pieces. Hmmmmm...Let's discuss this, son, please?

My other issue is when you have told your son to go and shower, they supposedly shower and when they come downstairs, they still smell the exact same way they did when you sent them to shower. Hey there, it's only been five minutes, you showered that quick? Did you wash everything? Did you use soap and water? Did you actually turn on the shower and get in? Did you get wet? Did you wet the towel and then rub it over your entire body? Did you wash in between your toes? You did? Well then why are your toes still black? Why do you have no wet towels in your shower? Why do you still feel sticky right here? Did you shower next door, because this shower in my house is still dry, almost like the water never got turned on but you are for certain it did, so let's assess. Why do tween boys avoid the shower? I know it's not because they don't want to be clean. I believe it is because they were asked to shower in between a live game and for some reason they can't just leave or they will die and, they can't die, they are too far along, and they are playing with a team. Oh Em Gee, I am so over this shit, just go wash your ass as I asked so I don't have to smell you all night?

Clothing selection gets me with boys. I have no idea how to deal with this issue most days. Some days I think it is getting better and then he does something that shows me I was crazy for thinking that foolish thought. You have a hamper in your room, right, son? Why don't you use it? I purchased two for you and you don't use either—why? Did you smell that before you put it on, son? Do you know if that is clean or dirty? How am I supposed to know what to wash? Why did this basket still have dryer sheets in it? Did you bring me the clean clothes to wash all over again? Where is your belt, son?

What do you mean, you don't have any belts? Shit, we have a belt thief then, because you had ten belts last week when I was in your closet putting your clothes away, so where did they go? Why do you have on mismatched socks, buddy? All of your socks were paired together, because I did it for you, so we don't keep having this issue? Why is your underwear on backwards and inside out? Did you not see or feel the tag? Do you not even care? Do you even know if those are clean?

How is it that when they get to high school, all of a sudden, their sense of style changes drastically. They start caring about how they look and what they smell like. They get upset when we walk behind them and question them about deodorant, clean socks, clean undershirts and underwear. They actually would like to have their clothes pressed and ironed. They seem to take better care of those expensive-ass shoes and clothes. Things just seem easier and we are so happy until we find out the reason all of these changes have come to fruition: a girl. Oh, no…you are my baby and my baby only. Tell her to find her own little boy to smile at. Those kisses belong to his mama, so back up or get backed up unapologetically. I can't even discuss this topic, because it makes me sad to think that soon, very soon, his hugs, kisses, cute smiles and laughter will all be given to someone other than me. I can't deal, so let's not and say we did. These little girls better get to know me really quick because I don't play about my little boy. I can tell you how to #SURVIVE the smells, dirty clothes, farts, homework, tantrums, school and all of that other stuff, but what I am still trying to learn how to #SURVIVE is my little boy turning into a man! #SURVIVIN' ain't easy, but it can be done. I am learning just like you all are, which is exactly what us moms need.

SURVIVIN' BEFORE SCHOOL
AND AFTER SCHOOL

SO AS MOMS, ONCE WE GET UP FROM OUR BEDS WE ARE immediately on duty until we lay our heads on our pillows and attempt to shut our eyes. From the time we wake up until the time we go to bed, it is nonstop strategizing, planning and organizing how to tackle the day and move onto the next one without incident and keeping everyone in one piece.

Let's start with the mornings. Our plans are always to get up and get OURSELVES together for the day, which involves many things like showering, getting dressed, doing our hair, ironing, putting on our fabulous face, giving ourselves a pep talk and actually walking into the hallway to activate the chaos. When my alarm goes off at five a.m., that is for me to start my daily routine for my self-care. My self-care plan does not include the kids or the husband, but it always ends up that way. I will be honest and tell you that out of a seven-day week I usually get my self-care time only one or two days, if I am lucky. Usually because either I know I had to do something in the morning for the kids for a project or homework, forgot to put clothes in the dryer before I fell asleep that are needed for that day or I just simply slept through my alarm or pushed the snooze button too many times and now I am behind schedule. It is usually the last two that get me off my self-care routine.

When I do laundry throughout the week, it's because P.E. uniforms need to be washed or we ran out of uniform tops for school because someone forgot to bring all of their dirty clothes to the laundry room. So that causes me to have to do laundry at night, and once I start doing laundry, I go hard. I started washing shit I had no intention of doing on a Wednesday night. Like, why am I washing comforters and sheets from the guest room when no one slept in there this week? Do we have company coming tomorrow? Why am I washing the kitchen towels used today for breakfast, lunch and dinner when there are only five of them? They can wait until Sunday laundry day, right? So, what happens is I ask the kids to get out their school uniforms for tomorrow and BAM, someone comes downstairs and tells me they don't have any clean tops or clean bottoms. Ummmm, how is that even possible because I did all of your dirty laundry on Sunday and today is Wednesday? How is that even possible because when I purchased your uniforms, I purchased six tops and six bottoms so that we had a grace period? How is that even possible, just how? They never seem to have an answer, but they always seem to have that look on their face that is lifeless and has no meaning. It's the most annoying face ever and I always get super-irritated and my blood pressure goes up really quickly. Oh, and they stay like that for like five minutes and say nothing, absolutely nothing. It's so fucking irritating, right?!

Anyway, I digress, so basically self-care time is a no go and I really have given up on it at this point. I just deal with the shit and move on about my day. OK, kids have been woken up, breakfast is done, lunch boxes are set and ready to go and everyone has on clean clothes, matching socks and you hope undergarments, but you don't have the time for that quality control check because you have three minutes to make it the car, seatbelts on, bookbags and lunch boxes in and out of the driveway to the first stop sign. You have all the confidence in the world your kids will not let you down today. They secretly know that if you are late today, you will be fired—well not really, but you have said it so many times that it is finally sticking in their little heads. You get in the car, do your quality-control checks, all looks well, kids are intact, and all are in their respective assigned seats. You put the car in reverse, praying silently the entire time that you make it out of the driveway. You make it—OMG you are on a roll today. You put it in drive and just as you floor the fucking gas pedal, someone in the fucking third row of the Suburban, yells, "Mom, I forgot my project upstairs!"

You hit the brake pedal so hard, all kids in seatbelts fly forward and at this point you are so pissed you forget to ask if anyone is hurt. You look into that rearview mirror, you adjust it so you see that kid and that kid only and you give them the look of death and all that comes with it. Then this happens: "WTF do you mean you left your project upstairs? What project? Did you not hear me say get all of your shit and get to the car? Did you not process that information? What were you doing?"

FUCK! FUCK! FUCK! Now I am really going to be late and I'm getting fired today. "Hey, you two better thank your brother, because now we will no longer have unlimited data because mommy just lost her job!"

So this starts a shit show in the car, the kids are yelling at each other and you are pissed that you have to turn around and get back inside your house, get the project from upstairs and back down again, all in two minutes so that you can get to work only ten minutes late, not twenty today. You haul ass back to the house, open the garage from down the street, disable the alarm code as you are driving (don't judge, we are on a mission here), take your seatbelt off halfway from your house, put the car in park while you are going up the driveway, jump out of car, run in house, go up the stairs seven at a time and you only have fourteen total stairs, grab the fucking project, jump down the stairs, run thru the kitchen to the garage door and your side mommy-vision eye notices a lunchbox on the counter and you grab that shit, and then you notice a bookbag by the door, so you grab that one too and hit it to the car. Throw the shit at all of them, seatbelt on, garage door closed, alarm armed, car in reverse and back to the road you go. You do all that shit in under two minutes and realize that you are the fucking boss and rock, but you also notice that you are sweating like you just worked out for an hour at SHRED 415 and today was your day off. Thankfully due to your good mommy sense, you have a full outfit with options in your gym bag in the trunk for days like this. You compose yourself, tell your kids to put in their AirPods and roll out while listening to your morning show and get yourself all the way together.

And that my friends is how we start our days as bad-ass moms, #SUR-VIVIN' mornings!

Now let's discuss the afternoons aka after school. I'm talking after the pick-up line, after any after school appointments and extracurricular activities, if any have been planned or scheduled for that day. I'm talking about pulling into your driveway and attempting to go in the house, after school. This part of after school takes a saint to #SURVIVE. It's dangerous, scary and exhausting at the same time. It is not OK for us to have to endure this type of climate daily, but I guess this is what we signed up for when we became parents.

So, we pull in the driveway and open the garage. We take a deep breath because we know that the shit is about to hit the fan when we open that door. They have been so quiet on the forty-minute drive home that you almost forgot you had children in the car and that they belonged to you. You know that this will not last much longer and you really want the quiet time even if that means you have to be with them for that quiet time. The car ride home is like a sanctuary compared to the actual home itself. It's HELL! It's the Devil's ass! It's not what you want at all! You can't back out of the driveway even though you have thought about it twice since pulling into your street. You can't do that because for some strange reason, they will all start screaming simultaneously at you, "Mom, where are you going? We want to go home. Why are you leaving again? Noooo, I want to go inside, I'm tired mommy!" Pause, insert the "What the fuck are you tired from face" and your side of HARD side-eye. Seriously, we all know that they are not tired at all. If they were really as tired as they claim, then they will walk in this house, put their shit down and retreat to their beds and fall the fuck asleep, but they don't, so why lie about it? Why would you even think that I would fall for that shit. I'm smarter than you kids. I'm a mom, it's my job. I'm smarter than a fifth grader most days of the week with proper sleep and care. Anyway, you fucking pull in the driveway, go into the garage and turn the car off.

Three…two…one…those kids get out of those damn seatbelts and into the house before you can take the keys out of the ignition. If only they moved this fast to get ready for school, you would never curse them out from six to seven a.m. daily. By the time you get inside the house—because it takes you a good thirty minutes to collect the grocery bags, your gym bag, and the lunchboxes and snack wrappers from the second and third rows, you get in the house and you have a wonderful surprise waiting for you. You didn't notice because for one you didn't check your planner and for two you were too busy daydreaming about pulling back out of the driveway for a few more minutes of peace that you totally missed the car in the driveway belonging to their damn DADDY!!

Daddy's home! Yes Lord! Thank you, Jesus! Daddy is home from work today and he can help you out tonight. Maybe just maybe you will get a good night's rest. You look up to the heavens and thank all your angels shining down on you today! Tonight, will be a good night! Daddy helps me and I will help him! So, you go in the house and you are expecting a hug and a kiss from your doting hubby and all you see is bags on the floor, refrigerator wide open, cabinets raided, shoes in the hallway and three kids chillin' on the couch with their iPads, all saying simultaneously as you evaluate the F7 tornado damage, "MOM, we are hungry, what's for dinner? We are starving. How long will it take you to cook?"

That WTF look comes back again and you don't even think twice about it and you yell all the way from the kitchen to wherever their DADDY is, "HELLO HUSBAND!"

He comes out of his room and says, "Hey there! What's up! How are you doing?" You look at him with zero words and the face of "you know how I'm doing, so stop asking!" but you say, I'm good, but can you help me tonight?" Those kids who are on the couch on their iPads who belong to you, say again, "Mom, we are hungry, like starving, what's for dinner?"

Their daddy notices that you are about to silence a kid or two, so he jumps in and says, "Hey, how about I make dinner and after dinner we go out for ice cream. But I have to get a few things done for work, but I will be right out!"

The kids, who again, belong to you, look at you like, mom WTF does he mean he will feed us, but he has to do work first, we ain't got the time or the patience for that, feed us NOW!! You have seen that look way too many times, so you know exactly what is about to happen in T minus five minutes. The mega fucking meltdowns about hunger will start, which bring whining, complaining, crying, complaining and more whining. You do a quick debriefing in your head about the most recent actions that have occurred since you have been inside your house for twenty minutes.

That quick debriefing provided you a moment of sincere clarity and wisdom. You drop the shit you were still holding onto and you yell for their DADDY. He comes out and you say very quickly but, in a stern, but nice voice, "I need to go to the gym for my work out because I didn't get to go this morning because we had a lot going on while trying to leave the house. There are leftovers in the fridge, the keys to my car are on the counter and I will be back later!" You grab your already pre-packed emergency gym bag, grab his keys, run out the garage door, open the garage, run to the front of the house where his car is parked, jump in the front seat, start the ignition and Thank the good Lord for a circle driveway so you can just hit DRIVE and HAUL ASS without looking backwards. You are going 60 mph down your own street that has those signs that say, "Drive Like Your Kids Live Here" and you are the one who put those signs up, but you say, "FUCK THAT," I'm out. You get to the stop sign, hit a left, then a quick right and just like that you are too far away from home for anyone to run and catch you.

You take a big deep breath, mostly because your watch says "BREATHE" and you pull over really quickly to use your phone. You unlock your phone, go straight to your app and sign your ass up for two classes back to back 5:45 and 7:00 p.m. at your favorite stress reliever, SHRED 415! You get the "SUCCESS, you are now signed up for Butts & Legs." And just like that you got the peace and quiet that you have been daydreaming about, but this peace and quiet comes with a little Reggaeton, Hip-Hop and Oldies Jamz, all while preparing your mind and body to hit that 12% incline on Butts and Legs day! You finish your sign-up and you start to pull off, but you realize you need to get your workout started in the car by moving your arms and abs from side to side! So, you cue up some Biggie Smalls, a little Snoop Dogg, a smidgen of OutKast, few hits from J and Bey, Usher and your oh so favorite Maroon 5, all so you can get into your BAD ASS MOM, SURVIVIN' LIKE THE BOSS I AM, ALL I DO IS WIN WIN WIN type of vibe and ROLL the HELL OUT, with your shades on, sunroof open and music blasting! The last thing you say as you hit that corner going a cool 30 mph is… "Today was a good day and I #SURVIVED!" in your Ice Cube mama voice!

SURVIVIN' FAMILY TRIPS BECAUSE LET'S BE CLEAR, IT'S NOT A VACATION

YES, YOU READ THAT RIGHT, IN MY HOUSE WE DON'T call them vacations because they are NOT vacations. Let me break the Word "VACATION" down for you really quick. A "VACATION," according to dictionary.com, in the NOUN form means a period of suspension of work, study or other activity, usually used for **rest**, **recreation** or **travel**; recess or holiday. It can also mean, **freedom** or **release** from **duty**, **business** or **activity**. Let's discuss how this word doesn't mean SHIT in my house at this current time. Please read below and you will soon start to realize that this definition does not apply to families with kids. Honestly, it should be banned when you are using it to describe a time away from your home with your kids.

Planning a family "vacation" is not easy. I am sure that most of you start your planning process the way I do. It is not easy and can be quite stressful, but we #SURVIVE this stage because we have one rule and that's, don't tell anyone about what you are doing until you are done doing it. That way you don't get unsolicited or unwarranted requests from anyone. The first thing I do, as I know some of my girlfriends also do, is load up that school calendar, and I take out my planner and ask my husband for his work calendar, so that I can start looking at days that we ALL have off. This isn't rocket science for most moms because no matter what you think you want to do that works best for your sanity, it always will happen either during winter break, spring recess or summer break. We love to look at all the months on the calendar like we have options. Why we put ourselves through that I have no idea. I am so guilty of saying, Fuck that, it's more economical for us to travel to Thailand in February, but who the hell is missing school for two weeks because I want to save money? Not me, I might talk a good game, but we aren't missing school for a "vacation," because for one thing, I don't have time for the missed assignments and projects. Also, it definitely won't be a "vacation"—nothing will be relaxing with a twenty-two-hour plane ride that leaves at one a.m. with four stops and three kids and a husband. In addition, I really can't take off work in February anyway. But it's the thought that counts, right? In my house we are going either during spring recess or summer break.

So now the next step, once you decide on a time period, and potential dates, you need to choose a location. This is where the "vacation" planning starts to fuck with your psyche. I have three kids—one nineteen-year-old and two thirteen-year-olds, so when we pick a place to "vacation," I spend time making sure that all of them will enjoy the destination, because who cares where I want to go. No one cares—NO ONE, sis. All they worry about at the stage my kids are in is "I wonder if there will be good SnapChat filters and if I will get good Instagram pictures. Mom better choose a good place this year." My girlfriends have younger kids, so they have to make sure that all activities at the location will wear their little asses out. Picking a place to "vacation" is not easy at all. Kids make everything more difficult because there are too many factors. I look at all my options carefully. I am glued to my laptop and I usually have six to seven tabs open up ranging from travel booking sites, to reviews of the hotels, to what things to do in the location, oh and the most important one is the Google search results of "family friendly vacation spots." The search for the perfect Walker Family "Vacation" is not a game.

When I started looking for locations last year, we needed to get away from it all over here on the East Coast. We needed a reset and a chance to really feel like we were away from it all for just a moment. So, the location search was centered around the West Coast. I was initially looking at California, but when I was searching for the perfect places to visit in hot-ass July, it just so happened that at least two earthquakes hit Cali days apart, so I scratched Cali off the front runners. Next on the location list was Arizona—Phoenix, to be exact. I have friends there who have teenagers my twins' age, but no one for my oldest to hang out with. OK, we can still work through that, so I proceeded to start planning. I was looking at hotels that were family friendly, which we all know is code for full of shit for kids to do activities. I found a great hotel and it checked off everything on my list. Next up was "things to do in Phoenix." So many things to do in Phoenix that looked exciting and great, but one problem I ran into was thinking about how all three of my kids would be entertained at the same damn time. Then the hubby throws a curve ball and says, if we are going all the way to the West Coast with the kids, we need to take them to see the Grand Canyon. I wanted to scream, because that meant that the itinerary I was building needed a major overhaul. Yes, we could definitely go to the Grand Canyon from Phoenix, but the drive alone would eat up an entire day and I ain't got time for that. I am not going on "vacation" to travel within my travel. Nope, I'll pass.

At this point, Arizona was officially crossed off and I needed to readjust my search criteria to include, family friendly, Grand Canyon accessibility, great hotels and good food. Drum roll please………. The list was down to its last contender. Las Vegas, Nevada. Yep, I was taking my thirteen-year-olds and nineteen-year-old to Sin City and I don't care what you think. It checked off all spots on my list, and that is all that matters. Planning a "vacation" to Las Vegas for a family of five in July was not too hard. Why? Because there are many family-friendly hotels, great food, amazing and most importantly FREE activities, the Grand Canyon and a bonus spot, the Hoover Dam, and it was a three-hour time difference from home so we definitely should be able to hit RESET. I told the hubby and the first thing he said was, "Vegas, with the kids? How is that gonna work?"

I was so prepared for that and all he needed to hear were two simple phrases: Baby we are UNDER BUDGET, AND the flight is NONSTOP. SOLD, to the man over there pulling out his credit card and screaming BOOK IT NOW!!"

In less than fifteen minutes, the Walker Family "Vacation" to Las Vegas was booked for a family of five from Miami. Excursions to the Grand Canyon and Hoover Dam, booked! Family-friendly hotel on the Las Vegas Strip, booked! Let me also point out that I used those built-up Hilton Points and we only paid for one night out of five! Don't sleep on those reward cards, ladies, RUN ME ALL MY POINTS PLEASE AND THANK YOU! I have a girlfriend who will literally call the hotels in her "vacation" location just to ask them if they will honor her Platinum status with Marriott. If they don't, they literally move to the bottom of the list. She also will fight to use her points at certain hotels, and when I say she will get all of her points back, if a cancellation happens, she gets ALL and then some back.

I never tell the kids where and when we are going until it has all been booked. I do this because the reaction is the same as when you tell them you are taking them somewhere; they really want to go. They will ask you every fucking day about it to the point you don't really want to take them or go any longer. It's so annoying, and I know you guys agree with me. That shit works my nerves. I understand you are excited, but it will not make it come any faster by asking daily about it. When I told the kids we were going to Las Vegas for a week, I was hoping for smiles, screaming, shit some sort of excitement, but all I got was, "Oh, why did you choose Las Vegas, mom? Don't you have to be twenty-one to do anything there? Isn't it really hot in Las Vegas in the summer? What hotel are we staying at, does it have a pool? What is there to do in Las Vegas, mom?"

I took a deep breath before I went full CTAY (Cuss They Ass Out) Mom. I have been working on my crazy, fucked-up outburst when my kids sound unappreciative of my time and effort when planning to take their complaining, nonworking, underage, can't take care of yourself asses somewhere. I calmly—but my face was saying an entirely different thing than my voice, but you get what you get at this point, take it or leave it—said, "Yes, it is very HOT in Vegas during the summer months. Yes, the hotel has a pool. Yes, there are many things to do in Vegas for people under twenty-one. I chose Vegas, because I chose Vegas. You can stay home and not enjoy a free trip or you can come with us and enjoy a free trip, but honestly, the only option you have is the latter, so I hope you enjoy it and don't give me attitude or it will be your last one on my dime. OK?"

I also decided to tell the girls, who really hate when I spring things on them last minute, because they somehow believe that they always need NEW "vacation" clothes when we leave, that we were leaving in two weeks and I'm not buying new clothes. Spend your own money. They all looked at me and said "Two weeks? Are we running from someone?"

I couldn't help but laugh, and said "No, you all know I will always find a deal and two weeks from today, we are out this Bitch. Oh, and we will be gone for five days and our flight leaves at eight a.m., which means we have to be at the airport by six a.m.!" That is the moment as a mom, you drop the damn mic and walk away. That was a full fucking WIN in my Mom book and the bases were loaded. In my head I am repeating to myself, in my Dorinda Medley voice, "I'm just trying to make it NICE!" Why do kids always complain about vacations when they are not paying for it? Does anyone have an answer for me? Anyone?

So how many of you start packing for your family "vacation" two weeks in advance? #RAISESHANDWITHOUTSHAME! The amount of checks and rechecks I do when packing for a family of five is not OK. The amount of travel-size lotions, toothpaste, hand sanitizer, wipes, body wash, shampoo and all things travel size, is not OK. I literally make about ten trips to Target's travel-size aisle before we depart. I make sure everyone has everything with extras. I pack each bag individually, so I know what is going inside. I know some of you are thinking, why doesn't she let her kids pack their own bags? I'll answer that for you.

I let my college kid pack her own stuff. She is an adult, but I do ask her at least 100 times, if she has every required item on my list, and once she rolls her bag to the hallway, which lets me know it's ready for a #momcheck, I will add shit if necessary. I really don't take anything out, because at nineteen you are set in your ways, but I will make sure all outfits are family-friendly appropriate! I DO NOT, I repeat DO NOT allow my middle-school kids to pack their own bags. They will have some input on clothing choices, but honestly, I take things out I don't like that they added in and I make sure all outfits are matching and in good condition. That's really for my son, because if I let him pack his own bag, all that would be in there are slides, old dusty-ass tennis shoes, white t-shirts and gym shorts. He only wants to wear gym clothes these days and it drives me insane. I am like, BOY, you have so many nice button-downs, great shoes, nice shorts but you chose to go to dinner in gym shorts and a T-shirt because that's your style. No, son, that's not your style, that's just being lazy. For his sister, I definitely let her have more say-so in what we pack, but she can be difficult, too. I just sit with her when packing, shake my head yes but that really means I will remove it when you are not looking or I will replace that entire outfit with one I like better and you will not even notice because the purpose of packing a bag two weeks in advance is so you don't remember what's in it until you open it and you are stuck with what inside! Yes, I pack my husband's bag, too. It's not that he is incapable of doing it. It's that he will ask me at least 100 times what he should pack and if this goes with that and he needs new underwear or new shirts.

Wait a second, I need to ask you all a question. Does anyone in your family feel like they need new underwear and undershirts to go on a vacation? Why are your current underwear unacceptable for travel? Why do I need to spend twenty dollars on a new pack of white T-shirts and a pack of new socks for you to feel comfortable with traveling? I do all the laundry and trust me; they are all clean and without holes. I only will pack the decent ones! LOL! It blows my mind but anyways, I pack his bag because if I didn't, I would end up doing it anyway and I have to make sure that he has all of his essentials just like the kids. Packing all bags is what makes me feel safe! Trust me, someone will forget something they swear they packed, and they didn't but I have my "extra's bag" with all the shit they always forget to pack. So, when I hear, "Mom, I forgot my charger! Mom I forgot my toothbrush! Babe, I forgot to pack no-show socks! Babe, did you grab the headphones I had on my nightstand? No, oh damn I forgot them then!" I just show up like Travel Claus and save the damn day and prevent an entire meltdown. I ain't got time for that shit. It's my "vacation" too, right? You will not stress me out, and we just got here! Again, don't judge me! It's part of me #SURVIVIN' this thing called a family "vacation"! Friendly reminder, the word "Vacation" means a suspension from work, usually for rest. Where is the damn rest when you have to pack and plan like this? But you still want to call it a family "vacation!"

When travel day hits, that's when the real stress comes into play. I have successfully fit five days' worth of clothing, shoes and accessories in five carry-on bags, because I refuse to check bags if I don't have to. My kids can't believe that I actually fit all their shit in and got it closed with only one try! Five o'clock in the morning arrives and I wake up all of the kids and politely tell them get up, get dressed, brush your teeth, grab your personal bag and head to the car. I also make sure to tell them NOT to forget their headphones, chargers and gum. The complaining starts and I give the death stare and keep it moving. Thankfully for them, we have zero fights and zero attitudes, which makes the car ride to the airport easy. My husband starts stressing out because we have to park at the lot adjacent to the airport and then take a shuttle to the airport, and he is not sure if we will have enough time. I am calm, cool and collective, because I have this all planned. I have the boarding passes saved in my wallet and I will airdrop them to each individual upon arrival at the security checkpoint. I have extra usb phone chargers in my purse along with airplane-friendly plug in headphones to watch movies on the plane, because we all know that the ones they provide never stay in our ears and trust me, one of my kids (kids includes husband) forgot one of those things at home or in the car parked at the lot. I also started looking at where we would go once we arrived to grab an Uber to the hotel. I also made sure to contact the hotel and use my nice words and friendly attitude to get early check-in approved! From my eyes, it's all good.

Going through security with the kids back in the day was a mission. We were always getting random bag checks because my kids always thought it was appropriate to bring scissors to do art on the plane, have food or drinks in their book bag or simply cry because they were scared to fly. As they got older, they were no longer scared to fly, and those random bag checks became obsolete and they learned that we could actually purchase food and drinks once we passed the security checkpoint. But for some reason, on our most recent trip through airport security, it was like a blast from the past. I had my son's medications in my purse, labeled and all and I still got a random check and asked several questions, like I was smuggling drugs for the cartel. That was just on the way there. On the way home, my oldest daughter's purse that had her camera inside, was missing. They had it go through the scanner, took it to the side to look in it for something they felt was suspicious, which was facial wipes, and then somehow, they never returned it to her. The frustrating part was that the man who took it, can't remember where he placed it when he was done looking through it. After several TSA agents later, we found ourselves six lines over confiscating our own bag, WTF! I also had to wait for them to call the CDC, I swear, that's who they called, to check out his medication again. I was so annoyed, and my kids were annoyed with me like it was my fault we were stopped yet again. So, what about that was relaxing, which is part of the definition of a "vacation?" I'll wait as you try to find the relaxing point within this situation. Yeah, you can't find it either, that's what I thought, but you still are using the word "vacation." I don't get it.

Arriving at your location comes with its own set of shit. Everyone is tired, everyone is hungry, and everyone just wants to get off the plane in five minutes or less. As a mom, we better be able to locate each overhead compartment that is housing your party's luggage. We better have the Uber app loaded and ready to hit "FIND." We better make sure the hotel is still going to honor our early check-in or this shit will go from 10 to 1000 in less than three minutes. Once you arrive at your hotel, you are praying that all goes well with the check-in. You make sure that everything you saw on their website was legit. Is the pool really that nice? Do they actually have a gym that overlooks the city? Are the waters really free? Once you get off the elevator and start rolling your luggage down the hallway with four judgmental people right behind you, the anxiety is building up inside you because you chose this hotel. You saw the room on the internet and compared it with at least 200 other ones and you chose this one. Is it really as spacious as they show? Does it have that nice big bathroom, with nice big beds and the amazing view the reviews claimed it had? The room key goes in, the green light and chime turn on and you open the door with hesitation but with excitement at the same time. O M G, this room is amazing. The beds are big! The bathroom is amazing, and that view is everything. They have no reason to complain about this room, but I'm sure they will find something they don't like. How can they not, it's in their kid DNA.

The next phase of a family "vacation" is starting the FUN! That includes going out of the hotel room and exploring the city you decided to spend five whole days with your family in. As moms, we already have a pre-planned itinerary based around everyone's wants, needs and desires. You have one that really doesn't want to have a history lesson while on "vacation." You have one that wants to go on an eating tour for the entire five days. You have one who will pretty much do anything without too much complaining, and you have one that is so indecisive on everything from food to activities and their answer is always, "I don't care but…." Uuummm, excuse me for pointing this out, but that means you care, and I need a solid yes or no so I can take an accurate count, and majority rules in this house. Long story short, I have no idea why we take the time to make itineraries or plan out activities for our families to enjoy as a group when it will end of being picked apart and we end up pissed because you were only trying to make it nice!

The days go by, and it's like you never left your house. The kids are fighting, no one can make a decision on dinner, we are going to be late as usual for our reservation time and mom is stuck with the heaviest bag with everyone's shit stuff inside. I don't know about you all, but I can't wait for this shit to be over and I can just go back home. It's like we never left our house, except we did, and we can't go back for another three days. You start praying that the trip turns around and you can just have five smiles that are actually enjoying the "vacation" you spent weeks planning and making sure it was as perfect as it could be. By the fourth day, they have no more fight, attitude or bad energy left, so you wake up to smiles, good mornings, and excitement for the day and most importantly good energy to take on the day. They are OK with whatever is on the agenda for the day; they all get up and get dressed without any arguments or complaints, and you realize at that point your prayers have been answered and you will get one day of peace! I mean, it's no secret that the reason everyone is "vacation"-compliant is because they know that tomorrow is boarding day and it's time to go home and the fun is about to be done, gone, obsolete! We can all honestly say, we don't care why they are being so great, we just want one day of peace! The day before the "vacation" ends is really the only day that may feel somewhat, almost, not really, but slightly, kind of a little bit, like a "vacation!" You get a little bit of relaxation, because there is no fighting. Rest may come to you unexpectedly because everyone will knock out early because all of the activities you planned for one day will wear their asses out. You definitely will have recreation because finally you get through one complete day of our jam-packed itinerary and last but not least, you will get a release from duty because no one will be asking you to do anything that they can do themselves because for one day, they are respecting the fact that you are on vacation with them so why don't we let mom enjoy her time, too.

So now that I have explained what a family "vacation" is for me, do you understand why I REFUSE to call it a family "vacation" and refer to it as a family trip! Let's remind ourselves of what the definition of vacation is. A "VACATION," according to dictionary.com in the NOUN form, means, a period of suspension of work, study or other activity, usually used for **rest**, **recreation** or **travel**; recess or holiday. It can also mean **freedom** or **release** from **duty**, **business** or **activity**. A "TRIP", according to dictionary.com in the NOUN form, means a **journey**, **voyage** or **run** made by a boat, train, bus or the like, **between two points.** Now if we really look at these two definitions and compare them to our own experiences of traveling with our families, there is a clear winner here. You can deny it if you want to, but it is what it is. When we travel with our kids, we get very little to zero, none, nada, REST, RECREATION, FREEDOM FROM DUTY, but the only thing you are certain to get 100% of is travel. You have to travel from your house to another location. In all seriousness, if you are traveling with you kids what you are really doing is taking a journey or voyage made by a boat, plane, train, car, bike, bus or whatever form of transportation you choose, to get between two points. Point A being your house and Point B being not your house! My friends, we have a clear winner here! Please, don't fight it. I know it sounds better and more sophisticated when we say we are taking a "family vacation." It looks good and reads well on Facebook and Instagram. We are moms, for us it is perfectly OK to say how we really feel and what is really going on. That's how we #SURVIVE this thing called parenting together. When we are real about what is going on in our daily lives as parents, we are not only helping ourselves, we are helping each other. So, do yourselves a favor when planning to travel with your family. Instead of saying "FAMILY VACATION" say "FAMILY TRIP." There is way more room for errors, and family trips allow for chaos. Vacations only really live up to their definition when kids are not involved. I have decided that if I want to travel with less stress when with my family, we are going on a Family Trip and that's just that and I know for a fact I will #SURVIVE and they will #SURVIVE ME SURVIVIN' THEM!

SURVIVIN' DA "RONA"

THE WORLD WAS TURNED UPSIDE DOWN WHEN WE heard that COVID-19 had made its way into the United States and now it's time to PANIC! When I tell you that this Coronavirus really had me re-evaluating my day to day, I mean I never thought that I would INVOLUNTARILY be my kids' mom, homeroom teacher, cafeteria worker, counselor, principal, secretary, security guard, PE teacher, art teacher, music teacher; math, science, social studies and language arts teacher; and Uber Eats delivery person between the hours of nine a.m. and three-fifty p.m. Monday thru Friday. I mean, did I miss the parental memo or survey asking us if we wanted to stay home with our kids and teach them all while we have to work? I will answer that for you: HELL NO! The only memo/survey I got, and I am sure you all got one too, was do I need a laptop at home for my kids to engage in distance learning? I have plenty of friends who are teachers and I always tell them that they are saints and have a special place in heaven waiting for them, and after the first week of that INVOLUNTARY side hustle that DID NOT PAY, I will give my spot up just for you guys to get in first! That was tooooo much for me, so I know it was tooooo much for you!

So initially we were asked to stay home with our kids for two weeks here in Miami, and the first week was right before our scheduled Spring Break and week two was during our Spring Break. After we get halfway through week one, we get the news that we will be out for another two weeks after the break is over. So, we were expecting at least four weeks of self-isolation, self, meaning with our kids, spouses, pets and a shitload of personalities and attitudes on the horizon. As far as school closure is concerned, it definitely was a rush job by the county and, district leaders and our teachers adapted the best way they could with no preparation and short notice. I applaud their hard work and dedication to doing all they can to make this work for every student and every parent. I am no teacher and I never intended to play one on TV or anywhere else but look at us now. Never say never!

My friends and I freaked out for a hot minute, got ourselves together and adapted the best way we could. I am sure 150% of the world can understand the freak-out when you have multiple kids and they are in different stages of their education. See, I have a college student and two eighth graders, so this hit is different at my house. I have a girlfriend who has a fourth grader and two sixth graders; and then I have another friend who has a Pre-K, fourth grader and sixth grader, so this isn't easy, and it definitely hits differently at their homes. Coronavirus 2020 was not coming to play any games at all. #SurvivinCoronaVirus2020 was exhausting, comical, delusional, gritty, attitudish, rewarding, challenging but most of all it really showed us that if we can get through this, we can get through anything. I have no idea how we survived, homeschool, cabin fever and social distancing. It was exhausting and my inner and outer gangsta were challenged and pushed to the maximum limit at times but I #SURVIVED. My girlfriends #SURVIVED. We ALL #SURVIVED, "all" meaning our kids and spouses also #SURVIVED.

So, this idea of distance learning was not what we expected it to be. We assumed that the students would be online with their teachers via some sort of platform, but NOPE, nada, that was not the case. The first week was more like learning the ropes and getting through one day at a time. MULTIPLE online communication applications and platforms were being used for students to get their assignments, but they were crashing by the second. It was bananas, and the amount of yelling and crying was unbearable at times. Emails were coming in daily about kids not logging in or completing assignments like every hour from every damn teacher and when you have middle and high school kids, that means you have six to eight teachers EACH, so let that marinate for a second or two.

My worst nemesis was those damn parent communication apps like Teams, Remind and Edmodo. I swear to you, I almost threw my entire iPhone out the second-floor window at one a.m. at least twenty times over this #Coronavirus2020 pandemic. What teacher is sending messages to students at one a.m.? Why are you even up? If you have that much energy, please put it into face-to-face meetings instead of asking me to do face-to-face meetings with my kids for all eight classes. That shit was unacceptable and crazy. I thought it was just me, and then I heard from some of my friends who were getting the same dings and shit all hours of the night and early morning. Do you think I care about what the assignments are for this week at two a.m. Saturday morning? It is the weekend, people, and NO one, I mean NO one, can leave their house, so we will all be ready for Monday when it gets here. I mean was there no way to schedule that message to go out at maybe seven Monday morning or maybe even at seven Sunday night? I am asking for a friend, and that friend is ME. I'm asking as nicely as I can at this point.

Now we have the assignments for the week, and we know what is due. We have read and reviewed the very specific notes and directions attached to this week's assignments. I am not sure who else was taken aback by some of the turn in directions, but just to be clear, it made my blood boil. Wasn't the entire STATE on a Stay-at-Home Order? Were printer paper and printer ink FREE during #Coronavirus2020? Why do we need to print it, do it, then take a picture of it, scan it, then email it to you for my kid to receive credit? Why is the amount of work for my child so long that they are literally doing work from eight in the morning until three-thirty in the afternoon five days a week? If I am working from home too, who has the time and money to spend hours on assignments with a fourth grader? Why are we printing shit that the teacher can't touch? Someone please explain to me why a teacher thought it was appropriate to ask the students to do a three-dimensional project for Science, and just in case you were wondering, NOPE, they were not presenting them to the class via any video conferencing app. Yeah I was flabbergasted too when my girlfriend told me about it. I guess they didn't think they had provided enough meaningless work to do for the week; shit, I don't know, and I am so glad I wasn't the parent who had to do yet another project and during #SURVIVINCORONA2020 days. Sis, that's rough, I'm sorry you were subjected to such nonsense. I am not sure I would know how to react to these requests. They seemed a little bit excessive to not only me, but my friends as well, and I will explain my point of why I believe they were excessive for all parties involved.

According to Dictionary.com, "excessive" is an adjective and means going beyond the usual, necessary or proper limit or degree; characterized by EXCESS; and excess also as an adjective means more than or above what is necessary, usual or specified; extra. So, let me try to break this down for you on why I think the amount of assigned work was EXCESSIVE for all parties involved, and all parties includes, moms, dads, grandparents, pets, teachers, tutors, neighbors, shit, the pool man even. So, there are five school days in a week, Monday through Friday regardless of whether we are at home learning or in a physical school building. Let's break down a normal week in school for my kids. When we get home from school and the chaos begins, my kids usually have one to two hours of homework a day for all subjects. They are on a block schedule so they may only have one or two core classes a day and electives the other periods. So, if you total that up for the week, they have an average of about ten hours of homework or studying a week for all classes.

Now, as I mentioned earlier, they are middle schoolers, so they have more classes, more teachers and more demands. When my oldest was in high school, she had about two to three hours a day, was also on a block schedule and that averaged about twelve to fifteen hours a week of homework and studying. Her course load was heavy and had many advanced classes, so it was not too surprising. My good girlfriend has one in elementary school, and when school was in, she had about one to two hours a night of homework and they have five CORE subjects and electives like Art, P.E. and Music. So, in a week she had a lot of homework as a fourth grader, but she is at a great school and they are very advanced, so this was expected and accepted. What is not acceptable or will be tolerated at all is the ART teacher asking for a drawing to be done. The drawing is done and turned in via a picture sent to an email address. The parent awaits their grade—I mean the student awaits their grade—and it turns out they got a "C." Yes, you read that right, a "C." Who the FUCK is giving out "C's" for ART during #CORONAVIRUS2020 right now? I know, my girlfriend's daughter's fourth grade ART teacher. She posted a message on one of those random-ass communication applications that read, please look at my drawing and do it exactly like this and also make sure you use crushed coffee grounds to get the gold look and send it to me via this app, not the one we have been using. That's not for assignments, it's only to communicate what assignments are and when they are due. Hold the phone and take my purse, because all of that is fighting words.

It's a PANDEMIC, lady, the entire WORLD is shut down and your simple ass is worried about some damn crushed coffee grounds. Are you sending a container of coffee purchased by your ass to my house via Amazon Prime? The answer is NO, right? That's what I thought. Do you not drink coffee at your house? No, OK, well I do and it's fucking ESSENTIAL and I ain't got none to spare. I need all my coffee, ma'am. I actually asked my friend if I could respond for her because I had a lot to say, obviously. My request was denied, but she did say she had ONE parent in the class who actually asked those questions I was asking, but in a way more professional tone than I did. LOL, I can't make this shit up, which is why I wrote this book; these people have no idea what it means to really #SURVIVE. Especially during the COVID-19 pandemic. Shit was getting real, real!

So #CORONAVIRUS2020 hits and we close schools and go right to a distance-learning model. So, every state, shit every county in every state, tackled the distance learning in their own way. Here in Miami, everyone was on a different page and in totally different genres. The private schools were ahead of the game—expected, no one was shocked at all. They didn't really have a break in learning at all. The teachers and students immediately tran-

sitioned to Virtual Classrooms with regular school hours. When I say VIR-
TUAL, I mean VIRTUAL. Those babies had to get up and be ready for the
first period by the start of school, no exceptions. Traffic couldn't be used as
an excuse right now. What, did you have a jam at the brush-your-teeth sta-
tion? Well, get up earlier. NO one wants to hear it. You are Late and no your
mom cannot write you a note. I mean, it seemed seamless looking from the
outside in. The Charter schools were right behind the private schools and
started their virtual classrooms about two weeks into the closing of schools.
They trained their staff and teachers and the kids didn't seem to miss a beat.
Public school took a whole different approach to this distance learning model.
Now I am NO teacher nor do I want to be one or play one on television. I
respect teachers, but I also am a parent and some things are just not OK on
the parent level.

The first week was a bust; it was a learning game for everyone here.
Teachers, staff, administrators, district leaders, students and parents. Everyone was confused and trying to figure it all out as the days ticked by. About
three weeks in, they announced that two days at the end of a week would be
mandatory teacher professional development days. As a parent, I was excited,
because I assumed that the teachers were going to get more knowledge on
how to work through the virtual classroom and how to effectively use of the
technology we all have available to us during this time of remote learning. I
was not alone in my thinking; many of my friends, many people on Facebook
and IG that have their kids in the public schools were excited thinking that
they no longer had to Google how to do second grade science or high school
chemistry. I mean, this is what we were expecting since we heard of so many
people across the nation doing it this way. Well, just in case you don't know,
that was not the damn case. These teachers were taken away from our kids
for two whole days to come back doing the same shit they were doing before
the mandatory development.

So that following Monday, the kids log back in to all these damn applications and it's the same shit. I was hoping for at least a streamlined approach

with the applications. Is it too much to ask that we not have ten different apps to use? Why is it acceptable for each teacher to use different apps for each subject? Why can't the entire Math department communicate with one app and the science department chose an app they like? I know, let's make it simple for the parents and students, and every teacher uses the same application to deliver info and assignments. Think about it, a parent of an elementary teacher could have five to seven applications for one kid's teachers and maybe an additional two or three other ones that their other kid's teacher is deciding to use. And just to add insult to injury, each teacher has their own code for each class they teach. It's ridiculous and should be outlawed.

Why was the development not focused on how to create a virtual learning environment for your students? OK, OK, let me take a second and back up. My apologies, from what I understand, there were course offerings on how to use certain apps to create virtual classrooms, but the side hustle of not learning them, was amazing. I have no clear idea how my kids' teachers thought this shit was OK, but I was clearly not happy and accepted the fact that I was their teacher now and was not getting paid to do it and it was pissing me off each day. So, I guess the consensus with the teachers was let's make sure we do a virtual meeting at least once a week with each one of our classes. They only had "Office Hours" for three hours a day, which was basically the window you or your kids had available to them to ask questions. During those three hours is when they held their weekly virtual meetings. These were not virtual classes, like lessons were not being taught, work was not being reviewed, questions and answers about homework was not going on. The message sent to the kids on one of the 100 notification apps went a little something like this: "Hi, guys, so this week I will be meeting with my 'A' day classes on Monday, starting at 9:30 a.m. for period two, 9:45 a.m. for period four, 10:00 a.m. for period six, and 10:15 a.m. for period eight. I will be meeting with the 'B' day classes on Tuesday, following the same times for periods one, three, five, and seven. It will be a quick meeting for you to ask questions and we can have a little face to face if you want and feel free to turn your video and audio off, if you don't plan on speaking or want to be seen. I will know you are there by your name showing on the screen."

In my Kevin Hart voice, "Wait a minute, wait, wait a minute. First of all, you are not just gonna speed past that like you didn't just say what you just said." I need to assess this shit and break it down so I can get a better understanding of what you are thinking, because I am sure there is a reasonable explanation behind that comment. So, let me ask a few questions. Isn't the purpose of a video or virtual call for you to SEE who you are talking to? So, from now on when I Facetime my friends I should turn my camera off? If the answer is yes, then why the FUCK am I using Facetime when I can just dial their number? If you are just checking in to see if they have questions, why do you need to Zoom? If your Zoom chat will only be a few minutes, why are you doing it? What if the kids have questions on a specific math problem or science concept? Are you going to take the time to answer it fully, or will you just speed past that too and give some bullshit answer? Get out of your feelings and don't shoot the messenger. I am just asking for a friend, and YES, that friend is me, my friends, my friends' friends, my friends' friends' friends, and all the other people who are as confused as I am appalled at the audacity of that comment.

Can someone please help me understand the actual purpose of why they didn't just cancel the entire school year and take the time to get all their ducks in a row? I was so over people calling it distance learning because at my house, there were new lessons and concepts being learned with no teacher available in many subject matters. I know it may hurt some of my teacher friends out there, but really, the public school was a whole #SURVIVIN-MOOD daily. It was a struggle to get the kids and myself motivated daily. I am a public school kid, but honestly, this shit was a soup sandwich with soggy-ass bread and old meat. #SURVIVIN' #CORONAVIRUS2020 was not easy as a mom, dad, kid, teacher, grandparent, neighbor, shit it wasn't easy for anyone, but we #SURVIVED and we will continue to #SURVIVE as best as we can. If your kids and spouse are still intact, you were successful at #SURVIVIN'.

YOU WILL SURVIVE, I PROMISE

I WILL CONFESS NOW AND TELL YOU THAT THERE ARE sooooo many more subjects to talk about when it comes to #SURVIVIN', hence you would be reading forever and ever and ever. I know that being a parent/mom is so hard, but at the same time it's so rewarding. You get to create a mini version of yourself as many times as you would like! Life without kids can be challenging, but life with kids can be a nightmare most days and a picnic some days, but no matter what, all of our days in this thing called life should be Great and we should feel eternally Blessed.

As our children get older, we find ourselves laughing at them more for the shit they did as little kids, the tantrums they had as toddlers and the mood swings they had as they really started to grow up and become real little adults. We will find ourselves missing those moments when we had to make morning lunchboxes and do school projects. We will get sad when they no longer want us to pick them up in the actual pick-up line, because they prefer to walk two blocks over, but this way we still get that kiss from our sweet baby boys. We will reminisce about how many playdates we went to on weekdays and now all we do is drop off and pick up at this one's house, or that one's party. We will reminisce about all of the crazy car ride moments we shared with our kids, all of the morning fights and screaming because we are going to be late, because soon, very, very soon, those same kids that we rolled our eyes at, hid from in the pantry or laundry room, walked in late to your office because of, lost your voice from screaming their name during the biggest game of the season, made endless after-school snacks and lunch boxes that went uneaten, gourmet dinners that they hated, endless night runs to CVS, Walgreens or Target because someone forgot they had a project due in eight hours—those same kids will one day drive themselves to school, pack up their own lunch, take themselves to their own games or practices, drive to CVS, Walgreens or Target for the shit they need by tomorrow and we will not understand or accept that they no longer need us to #SURVIVE for them, they realize that they want us to #SURVIVE long enough to watch them go through exactly what we are going through. It's a beautiful moment but a sad and scary one at the same time. It's rewarding when you hear your kids tell you they Love you and you are the best parent ever! It warms your soul to know that you raised those babies to be the best humans possible. Today's world is full of disappointment, sadness, love, light, laughter and endless emotions to get us from day to day. All we can do as parents is give them the tools to be the very best version of themselves so they can pass that version on to their children and hear our children say to their children, "Now I understand!"

Forrest Gump said it best: "Life is like a box of chocolates; you never know what you're gonna get!" That is so true. We think we can plan how our life will be with kids, what type of parent we will be, how strict or lenient we will be, but in all reality and fairness, we do whatever our instincts tell us to in order to get by and #SURVIVE. If that means we may have to curse in the pick-up line a few days a week, or do a few school projects, sign up to be a room parent and we know we have zero time to do that shit, plan playdates, make gourmet lunch boxes and chef-inspired meals, at the end of the day all we are doing is #SURVIVIN' the day so that we can get to the next day, because what's most important is when we make it through one day with our kids we are so blessed to wake up to another day with our kids. Driving us crazy and to insanity is the reason they were brought into our lives. Without these little happiness-grabbers, what type of adult would I be right now? Not saying that if you don't have kids you will not be fulfilled, I'm only saying that when things don't go as planned, good things will come from it, it just might take fifteen to eighteen years, but it's all worth it! #SURVIVIN' is an art form and we are all capable of #SURVIVIN', we just need to always remember, we are NEVER ALONE, we always will have that fellow mom out there who has been through it, going through it or is about to head into it! They say it takes a village to raise kids; well it also takes a mom to teach a mom and a dad to teach a dad! If you read this entire comedic memoir on how my friends and I have #SURVIVED our kids, you are the real MVP and trust me, you will be just fine! Phone a friend when in need and if all else fails, go to the farthest corner in your house, sit down and pick a chapter of this book, read it, laugh out loud—really loud— read another one, laugh out loud again, get up and Try Again! YOU WILL SURVIVE, I PROMISE!

SURVIVIN' BECAUSE OF MY VILLAGE

I HAVE SO MANY "THANK YOUS" TO GIVE OUT AND I AM sure I will miss somebody, but those who truly know me and know my heart, will not be offended. I have been blessed with so many girlfriends along my journey called life. I have heard so many stories that were completely different from my own and so many that had me thinking we lived in the same house! Just knowing that my day was just as bad if not worse than the next mom, kept me going! I knew if they were not giving up, then I better not even think about it!

Writing this book has been so much fun and so rewarding at the same time. I don't regret anything that I have written because it's exactly how I feel, and I cannot apologize for my feelings. One thing that I do know is that being a mom is one of the very best parts of me and I love it, even though I want to jump off the roof of my Suburban face-first most days!

I would first like to start by thanking my Lord, Jesus Christ. Without him, none of this is possible. You have blessed me in many ways, and I am forever grateful for your everlasting love and favor. God is Good ALL THE TIME and ALL THE TIME, God is Good!

THANK YOU, MOM, MIL (mother in law), NANNY (grandmother) and my TETEs for teaching me how to be a mommy and how to never give up on being the best mom I can be no matter what life throws at me! Without their support, love and lessons, I would not be the mom I am today! Becoming a mom at nineteen was not easy, but having my family be right by my side and never walking away from me, is the best thing ever. I am eternally grateful for the life lessons each one of those strong women taught me and continue to teach me every day! A special Thank you to my Aunt Lynn, the creative one! Your love for the arts and creativity is why I love you and you inspired me to turn on my creative juices and let it flow! Thank you Mom, for never giving up on me and always letting me know that I will be ok. That life may give me twist and turns but to always stay the course. Thank you Nanny! You are simply the BEST grandmother any child could ever ask for. You pray for me every day. You love me endlessly and you have always been right by my side thru each and every journey I have embarked on! Love you Nanners!

I know my MIL is looking down on me and smiling all while saying to her friends and family in Heaven, "That's my DIL and I am so proud of her, now go download her book so we can read it together!" I miss her with my entire heart, and I know she is so proud of me! Thank you, Beverly, for sharing your stories, love, support and most importantly, your Son!

To my SILs, Thank you! Ingrid, thank you for sharing the DIL title with me! Laughing with you is so much fun when we get together and you are such a kind soul. My babies love Anni Ingrid! Abby..ABby...ABBY! Thank you for being the best SIL ever! My babies are your babies and that's just that! Between our crazy emoji-filled text messages and love for creating new and exciting dishes for the next get-together...having you in my life is nothing short of amazing! You ride for me as I ride for you and that's just that!

To my cousins Alexis, Ashley, Jasmon and Tonya, this one's for you! Alexis, you may not have any babies, but my babies, Ashley's babies and Jasmon's babies have always and will always be your babies! You are the best version of a surrogate mommy we all needed as we learned how to navigate the streets of mommy hood at very young ages! We can't thank you enough for loving our babies as much as, shit, more than you love us! Ash and Jas, my heart always beats for you two! You two will always have that special place in my heart! You are more like my baby sisters than my baby cousins. I love you both so much and I am so proud of the wives, moms and women you are becoming! T, having you in my life has been so great! I have more than a cousin in you, I have a big sister! I have a friend! I have love! Thank you for your wisdom and your love! Thank you for just being you, T, a bright light in anyone's day! I love you and I can't wait to celebrate this journey with you!

I have to thank my babies, my heartbeats, the loves of my life, Lauryn, Liyah, Levar Jr. and Marquis! Lauryn, you made me a mom first and taught me the true definition of endless love! You have been by my side cheering me on since day one! Your drive for life keeps me going and I thank you! Liyah and Levar Jr., my Easter Eggs, you came into my world and made it so much better than it already was. You two brought chaos and curiosity, but you also brought a sense of calm to everyday because you two beat all of the odds and are true warriors in this place called life! The two of you are amazing little humans and will make the world a better place! Marquis, my bonus baby, I love you and I am so proud of the dad you are becoming! Thank you for allowing me to be a part of your world and loving me! I am the mom I am today because you all have taught me how to love unconditionally, how to be gentle and kind, how to be patient and how to be crazy in public and private. You have never given up on me! I am so blessed to call you my children and I thank God every day for choosing me to be your mama! I love you so much it hurts! My heart beats extra beats just for you! Mommy loves you forever and a day through infinity! I SURVIVED you guys, that is amazing! Can I get an AMEN!!! Let the Chuuuurrrrcccchhhh say AMEN!!

To my girlfriends, Wow, thank you all for believing in me! For pushing me to write this book! For keeping me laughing day in and day out with endless stories filled with tears, anger, laughter and most importantly love!

Monica, you truly are my inspiration for this book! Meeting you eight years ago has to be one of the best things EVER. We have so much in common, it's scary! It's our island and we will do whatever we want to on it! Tami, Marhonte, Kevia, Sascha—you ladies are the best! You have been nothing short of great girlfriends when a mama needs to vent! You not only can relate but you always seem to top my story or experience! Going through this journey called mommy hood with you guys has been so amazing and I am truly honored to call you my friends!

Thank you, Katie and Robyn, for dedicating your time in reading the book first! The feedback you ladies gave me was much appreciated and honestly, I drafted about fifteen extra pages based on your suggestions. It means so much to me that you carved out time in your busy days to help me, and I love you both for that! Angel, my personal Angel, my first best friend, my forever best friend, I love you and that's just that! We have been through so many of life's journeys together and I am so thankful for that. Being my best friend for over thirty years is simply the best! For all of my mom friends on social media and in life, thank you for just sharing your stories with the world day in and day out so all of us moms don't feel like complete assholes when we find ourselves arguing with our mini-selves! This book is for you! All of you, and I hope you enjoy it!

Levar Sr....my protector! My baby's daddy! The love of my life! The one who makes me crazy, but I can't be crazy for anyone else! Thank you for always supporting my crazy ideas. From my fashion shows to becoming an author, you have always been right by my side without doubt or fear. My ride or die. I may not always show it or say it, but I need you DAILY, just for me to know my life is OK! You are such a great daddy and our babies are so blessed to have you! When God put us in each other's path fifteen years ago, it was not by mistake, it was by design. It didn't hurt that you had water glistening all over your body on a hot summer day in Miami! I'm just saying, the visuals were key! Seriously, we get on each other's LAST EVER-LIVING NERVE, but we were designed for each other and I could not do life without you! As Neo says, "I'm in a movement by myself, but we're a force when we're together!" Thank you baby for doing this thing called life with me! I love you deep into my inner soul where no other can live but you! When I close my eyes at night and wake up to see you there, my world is not only OK, it's perfect in every single way!

Again, I say THANK YOU to everyone who has been a part of my journey as a woman, mom and wife. I love you all so much! I leave you with this...Life has thrown us all so many curve balls that we try to make contact with. Sometimes we have a strike, sometimes it's a foul ball but many times, it's a HOME RUN. One of my all-time favorite quotes is from Forrest Gump, and yes, I know I have already mentioned this, but here it is again—as I said, it's my favorite quote. "Life is like a box of chocolates. You never know what you're gonna get." My takeaway from that quote is this, it's a box filled with chocolate. Some of them you will like, some of them you will love, but all of them belong to you to do what you want with them when you want and how you want. You can enjoy them, you can cry over them, you can laugh at them, but no matter what, the decision is yours to make. When you are provided that box of chocolates, you will not know what types of chocolates are in that box called life, but I can assure you as long as you open that box and do what you want with that chocolate, you will be just fine. Like my MIL always said, "Les, be happy! Trust God! Have faith! Enjoy your life!" That, my friends, is exactly what I am doing! I am being happy! I am trusting God! I have so much faith! I am enjoying my life!

Being a mom is one of the HARDEST jobs on the planet! Being able to love unconditionally is a truly amazing feeling! Going from zero to one hundred in half a second because somebody is messing with your baby, is a BOSS move! Being able to answer three different questions, make three different meals, answer the phone, check homework, check teachers, schedule playdates, draft rough drafts for the science fair project and still manage to keep a smile on your face even though your boss has warned you that you cannot be late again or else...is BEING A DAMN GENIUS IN ONE OF THE MOST PHENOMENAL ARTFORMS, AND THAT, MY FRIENDS, IS EXACTLY WHAT SURVIVIN' IS. By any means necessary, we will SURVIVE and keep moving like nothing happened. In my inner Snoop Dogg voice, "It ain't nothing but a Mom thing, Baby!" SURVIVIN': IT'S JUST WHAT WE DO!